MW01264855

QUITTING

PLACES

CAMERON GIOVANELLI

GOSPEL PRESS PUBLICATIONS

COPYRIGHT 2013 ©

Printed in the USA by
FBC Publications & Printing
Ft. Pierce, FL
www.fbcpublications.com

ISBN NO. - 978-1-60208-338-7

Gospel Press Publications
A Ministry of Calvary Baptist Church
7321 Manchester Road
Dundalk, MD 21222
Phone (410) 285.4129
www.cbcdundalk.org

CONTENTS

3

DEDICATION

WHEN ASKED to whom I would like to dedicate this book, I did not have to think twice. This book is lovingly dedicated to my wife, Sarah Giovanelli. Many will never know the strength that my wife has found in the Lord during the difficult times of my health. I thank the Lord every day that it is I who is sick and not my wife or children.

Sarah, I am so glad that the Lord brought you into my life. Thank you for marrying me. Thank you for your patience with me when I was lost in thought over what the doctors had said. Thank you for never complaining about the hours and hours of doctors visits. Thank you for staying by my side while I lay in hospital beds. Thank you for taking care of the children and the home when I could not help. Thank you for holding my hand when I was scared about the next step. Thank you for allowing me to be a pastor and for being a wonderful first lady. Thank you for being my *completer* and not my *competer*. Thank you for being a godly mother. Thank you for being my wife. Who can find a virtuous woman? By the grace of God – I did!

SPECIAL ACKNOWLEDGEMENTS

To the wonderful people of Calvary Baptist Church – thank you for your patience and support during the quitting places of my life. You are the best people I could ever dream of pastoring.

To the pastor who is reading this book – I have been there! I have been there more than once! Whatever you are going through today, always remember, God will never give you more than you can handle. You are not alone when it comes to the quitting places in your life.

To the individual who is facing the quitting place in your life: I promise – if you will make it through this quitting place, you will rejoice over your decision for the rest of your life.

INTRODUCTION

A S A YOUNG MAN, I remember listening to Dr. Larry Brown while he was preaching at a conference. During his sermon, he made a statement that has stuck with me ever since: "Make it through the quitting places." There was far more substance to his powerful message; but for me that night, that statement is what the Lord impressed on my heart.

As the years went on, I would use that phrase when counseling and trying to encourage those that were seeking help for various situations. Over the last many years, I have found that *giving* counsel is far easier than *living* counsel.

In 2008, when I was diagnosed with kidney cancer, I was shocked! I had been in hospital rooms with those who had been diagnosed with cancers of all kinds. I have stood by others who had lost family members to cancer. During those times, I would do everything I could do to encourage them to "make it through the quitting places" in which they had found themselves.

A while back, a pastor called me and asked, "What do you feel the role of the pastor really is?" (Now, I would like to say that I understand that the role of a pastor is far more than the simple answer that I gave him. I also believe that the role of the pastor has been embellished in the minds of pastors; and we, at times, make pastoring far more difficult than the Lord ever intended.) When the pastor asked me that question, the first thing I told him was this: "I believe one of the most important roles of the pastor is to help the people of God make it through the quitting places." To this day, I believe that to be true.

No man is an island, and I have not had this book put together because I feel like I have arrived! As a matter of fact, a reason for this book is I feel that too often we get so concerned about what others will think about what we wrote, how we wrote it, and what people will say about it. We have become so paralyzed by the fear of man that we are not used of God to encourage those who may need to hear or read from someone who can relate to their current situation.

At the writing of this book, it will have been almost one year since my last round of cancer surgeries. After my second surgery of 2012, there were many complications. My body has grown more tired, and my recovery has seemed to drag on and on. There have been many times during this year that I have felt that the Lord may be trying to show me that it was time to move on to the next thing in my life. Then, I grew very convicted and even ashamed that I would entertain such a thought. "What am I supposed to move on to?" I asked my flesh. I know that I am doing exactly what God created me to do. I know I am not doing it to the caliber that God desires, but that is why we are to keep walking with Him and serving Him. Thank God for His patience.

This book has been written and compiled following a Wednesday night series of messages entitled, "Making It Through the Quitting Places". After coming out of this last surgery, people would ask me, "Pastor, how do you stay so strong?" The sad fact is, I was not nearly as strong as they thought I was. Every day, for several weeks, I would go to the Lord and ask Him to help me make it through this quitting place in my life. As I would read the Bible, the thoughts of this book are the thoughts that the Lord gave to me.

I am so very grateful for the patience of our wonderful Lord and Saviour – Jesus Christ.

PART I

LOOKING IN THE RIGHT DIRECTION

"I will lift up mine eyes unto the hills, from whence cometh my help."—*PSALMS 121:1*

DIRECTIONALLY CHALLENGED

D IRECTION IS KEY in a quitting place. Throughout the Bible, God often references the specific direction someone is looking. God still notices today. He especially takes note of our direction during our low times, for the direction we are facing during those times is paramount.

Psalm 121 is my favorite chapter in the Bible. Throughout my life, I have claimed it many times. In its verses, the psalmist shares how he made it:

[1] I will lift up mine eyes unto the hills, from whence cometh my help.

[2] My help cometh from the LORD, which made heaven and earth.

[3] He will not suffer thy foot to be moved: he that keepeth thee will not slumber.

[4] Behold, he that keepeth Israel shall neither slumber nor sleep.

[5] The LORD is thy keeper: the LORD is thy shade upon thy right hand.

[6] The sun shall not smite thee by day, nor the moon by night.

[7] The LORD shall preserve thee from all evil: he shall preserve thy soul.

[8] The LORD shall preserve thy going out and thy coming in from this time forth, and even for evermore.

No doubt, as David was penning this psalm, he was going through a trying time. He needed help. Time after time, David received the help that he desperately needed. How? I find that he started by looking in the right direction (verses 1-2).

I am often reminded of this "direction principle" when I go to Lancaster, Pennsylvania (Amish Country), with my family. It is not unusual for us, as we drive through those country roads, to spot horse-drawn carriages and horses with blinders. The blinders focus their attention. The goal is to keep the horses from looking to the left or to the right. Focused direction eliminates distraction. Without the blinders, the sight of passing cars could scare the horse. Noisy distractions could cause the horse to buck and possibly hurt the family in the carriage.

No, God does not want us to have physical blinders on. However, He does want us focusing on the right direction. He wants us to have self-control – to look in the right direction when it is crucially needed.

So often, Christians are terrified because we are looking in all sorts of different directions. Our eyes tend to wander. The result is the possibility of hurting ourselves and hurting those we are leading.

The terrified look comes from not focusing in the right direction. The same is true for the downcast look.

It is so easy to catch yourself with a downcast look when you are sickly. I am sickly. At the time of this writing, I do not think I have ever been sicklier. I am able to arrive at the church office at about 10:30 a.m., and I leave at about 5:00 or 5:30 p.m. When I get home, I am physically worn down – that is all the fuel I have in my tank. There can be nothing more frustrating. At age 35, I now come home worn out and many times not even hungry.

I cannot give the hours that I would like. I remember arriving at the church early, staying late – even going all night. I would be on the phone until late into the evening. Now, I am up in the early morning hours, but it is not because I am counseling. It is simply because I cannot sleep. My body just seems to be out of sync. There are so many opportunities to be downcast.

This book might find itself in the hands of one that has it far worse than I. In some cases, I am preaching to the choir on this subject. I am writing, though, from the heart of a 35-year-old preacher who loves God, who loves the people of God, and who has had a lot taken away from him over the past several weeks.

It is in these times that it is essential that I am looking in the right direction. When I look up (not looking all around or looking down), I am able to learn the lessons God is trying to teach me. I have learned a lot about patience. I have also learned how God has, through these times, brought our family closer together. I have learned the major lesson that He is in control of everything and that without Him, nothing else really matters.

I want to make sure in my life, as David made sure in his life, when difficulty comes, that I am looking in the right direction. Otherwise, the lessons God is trying to get across will never be recognized.

Isaiah 40:26 reads, "Lift up your eyes on high, and behold who hath created these things, that bringeth out their host by number: he calleth them all by names by the greatness of his might, for that he is strong in power; not one faileth." The verse is talking about the Lord. When a situation is in His hands, "not one faileth."

The Lord does not know how to fail, and we must remember that! With that in mind, which direction should we be facing? So often when we are going through trying times, we look down and around instead of up.

THE PLACE OF MY HELP

L OOKING IN THE RIGHT DIRECTION is the starting point in the journey through the quitting places. But that is just the beginning. Now that we are facing due north, we can begin focusing our eyes on a particular *place*.

God is very specific in the place we must face. Back in Psalm 121:1-4 we find that we are to look "*unto the hills*, from whence cometh my help." (Emphasis added)

The crucial concept I must remember is that our Lord is the Lord of everything. He is not just the Lord of some things. He is the Lord of absolutely everything. We find in the Gospels that His place is high and lifted up. He is high and lifted up in all His glory; and in order to find Him, *I must search the lofty places.*

It is awfully hard to find God in the depths of our depression! The tragic irony is that the depths of depression is where we seem to need Him the most.

Why do we struggle to find Him there? The answer is that our attention is on the wrong place.

In the low places, I am not supposed to focus on the low places. I am supposed to remember that I am to "lift up mine eyes unto the hills." Why? That is the place of my help. The *lofty* places, not the *low* places.

As I lift my eyes up and see Christ, I cannot help but look at the heavens and enjoy His handiwork. When I look up at night, I see the stars thrown against the black velvet sky. When I look up in the morning, I see how God paints the skies with a beautiful sunrise. When I look up at noon, I see the beautiful clouds. When I look up and it happens to rain, even those raindrops are refreshing. God takes that wet rain and causes green grass to grow. That which falls from above is powerful.

Many have serious, legitimate reasons to be downcast. We have all gone through things that have caused us to look down for at least a little while. Sometimes, God will stoop down, and He will lift that chin that is falling. He will not merely lift it, but He lifts that gaze up *towards Him*. Sometimes, God sends someone else to help as well – someone else to say the right thing at the right time.

For me, sometimes God sends Mark, my five-year-old son, to help. Every once in a while, he will pay me a visit by running into the living room while I am napping on the couch. I try to avoid lying down too much when the kids are home, so I make it a point to sit up when they arrive. Recently, the children came home to find me napping. When I sat up, Mark ran and jumped up beside me. He was eager to show me all the things that were new in his life. He began showing me things he colored and things he had found around the house. They were so cool to him.

We must have sat there for ten minutes, and I tried to be interested in all the little things he was showing me. Then, I started noticing that the household items he was showing me were some of the ones I had been missing! I said, "Son, where did you get that?" He simply said, "I found it." "Where did you find it?" I asked. It turns out that he had found it on my dresser. That led me to ask the more important question, "How in the world did you get up to the dresser?" He is five, but he figured it out. As I sat there with my son, I realized that to him there was not a care in the world.

Madeline, my ten-year-old, is our oldest and is also the resident comedian of the house. She will just say some of the goofiest things. It is total ten-year-old humor.

Then here comes Meredith, my second oldest, who is seven. Meredith loves to be girly and hates to get dirty. The mix of Madeline, Meredith, and Mark makes our house an extremely fun place to live.

My kids just want to wrap their arms around their mom and dad. They want to be loved and to hear, "I love you." I have found that I cannot be around my children and stay discouraged. It literally is impossible.

On top of all that, I have a very patient wife. She has shown tremendous patience, being my home nurse in recent days. She has shown patience with my recent wheel chair situation as well.

When I look at my wife across the dinner table, I do not see a discouraged face. She is not discouraged when we load or unload the wheel chair from the car. She is not discouraged when I have to stop and sit down for a few minutes. She always sits there with me, and we talk like everything is normal until I can get up and go again. We sit there as if our lives had entered the senior saint years. Every once in a while we will say, "Hey, you want to go and get a coffee?" That is code for, "I need to sit down for a minute." What used to take us thirty minutes to be done, takes us about an hour and a half now. We have not locked ourselves in the house either. We go grocery shopping together, we go to the mall together, and we have a good time. However, our lives have really, really slowed down. Though my life is in one of those midnight hours, my wife and I have no complaints.

I leave every church service with a smile. I leave on a higher plane than when I came. I enjoy preaching, but the message our church members preach to me (through their encouragement) is even more helpful.

I intentionally did not have handles put on the back of the wheel chair, because I did not want anybody pushing me. I determined that if I was going to be in this wheel chair, I was going to get all the exercise I could. Just recently, my brother-in-law and I went out for lunch and had a great time. There I was – rolling my wheel chair and having the time of my life. When we arrived home, I went to make a hospital visit. There I was again, sitting in my wheel chair, praying with one of our sick members. When Brother Hall (our Hospital Visitation Pastor) and I exited the hospital to the truck, he said, "Let me go get it, and I'll come down to get you." I told him, "That's not happening. Not a chance!" I raced him to the truck…and beat him to it!

Then comes those hours *when no one is around*. Madeline, Meredith, and Mark's sleepy heads have long since hit the pillow. Those are the moments where I am left with my own thoughts. It can be so dangerous. You can feel lost – reflecting on all that you have not been able to do that day. If I am not careful, even as a pastor, I fail to lift my eyes up *to the Lord*. It is in these moments when I must look toward the lofty places and say, "Lord, I don't understand what I am going through, but thank You for it." In the future, we will look back on *those* moments and remember them as the greatest lessons life has ever taught us.

THE PERSON OF MY HELP

T HANK GOD for the Person of my help! We understand that we must look in the right direction, but to whom? The following verses of Psalm 121 hold that answer.

> [5] The LORD is thy keeper: the LORD is thy shade upon thy right hand.
> [6] The sun shall not smite thee by day, nor the moon by night.

Though I have a wife that helps me, though I have children that help me, and though I have a church family that helps me, *nobody* helps me like the Lord helps me.

By the way, nobody helps *you* as much as your Lord helps you.

I can go to Him any of the 24 hours in the day. I can open the Bible to just about anywhere, and He will speak to me – giving me *exactly* what I need for that moment. All it takes is for me to go to Him.

In the late night hours and through the early morning hours, I can lay on the couch in my living room and just begin to pray. Tears roll down the sides of my head, hitting the pillow. I lay there talking to Lord, asking him for strength. Lately, when I am done praying, I *know* He has heard me.

I think that when we get to the point of brokenness and weakness, we *enjoy* talking to the Lord. I wonder that if those are the sweetest moments in my relationship with the Lord, then maybe that is why He has me going through this. Maybe if I am enjoying the sweetness of it all, then He might be enjoying it too. It is in the broken state that fellowship is very sweet.

Yet, our fellowship is not always that sweet. It is not always that sweet because we are caught up in the hustle and bustle of the day. Our lives start to roll so fast that we forget about Him. That is when the Lord has to sort of derail us for a little while. It is as if God says to us, "Hey, don't forget about Me."

When we are able to look back on those dark hours, we will realize how they were actually some of the brightest times. Why is that? Because you cannot go wrong getting closer to God.

A friend or a family member might not understand what you are going through. *You* might not even know what you are going through or how to explain the situation. You might not know how to voice your thoughts or explain what you are feeling. Know this: the Lord looks down, and He knows every thought. He knows exactly what you are facing. He understands. Before my friends can help me, before my family can help me, and before I can help myself, I must find my help *in the Lord.*

Maybe you are looking for an encouraging word from a mate. If that is the only person to whom you are looking, do not be surprised if you find discouragement. Maybe you are waiting for your child to say something funny to keep your spirits up that day. Do not be surprised if your child brings you heartache. If we cannot figure out how to get to God – how to find in Him what we are missing, seeking, and longing for – then how can we truly call ourselves children of God? As a child of God, I must communicate with my Father.

I could not even imagine if my children chose to ignore me when I spoke to them. I would not know how to feel if I said, "Hey, Mark, come here for a minute." and he said, "Not right now, Dad."

Recently, I called Mark as he was in hot pursuit of his sisters in the house. All I had to say was, "Hey, Mark, come here." I did not have to holler, and I did not even have to say it twice. He came right over and said, "Yes, sir." So, we started talking.

"What are you guys doing?" I asked him.

"We are going down to the basement. We're chasing Fred." Fred is the family cat.

"What are you trying to do to the cat?"

"Nothing."

"Mark, what are you trying to do to the cat?"

At that point, Mark started to get this weird look on his face. I knew I needed to pin him down for a few more minutes, because it may not be good down in the basement.

I have never had to argue with any of my children to get information out of them. I thank God for that. I have to think that our Heavenly Father is the same way. He does not want to have to do something drastic in order to make me talk to Him.

In a quitting place, let God have your undivided attention. We always have His. Do not waste what could be the sweetest time spent with God. Confide and rest in the *only* Person that can help.

THE PRESERVATION OF MY HELP

W HEN MY FAMILY lived in Visalia, California, every Saturday we would visit the Shelton's. It was tradition. Each Saturday afternoon we would eat lunch and have some type of cobbler that Mrs. Shelton would make for dessert. A couple of memories stand out about those Saturday visits.

For one, Brother Shelton would always be watching one of two television shows. He would either be watching The Weather Channel or "Big Hats" (the old westerns). Every once in a while, he would fall asleep watching The Weather Channel. We would take advantage of the opportunity and would switch the channel to the Big Hats. He would wake up about a half hour later and say, "Who changed the channel?" He would get all worked up and turn the television back to The Weather Channel. Then, about five minutes later, he would switch back to Big Hats like it was his idea.

The other memory, though, of the Shelton house was Mrs. Shelton's preserves. An entire wall in her breezeway was filled with all sorts of foods in jars. She would spend hours upon hours each year preserving. She preserved just about everything – apples, pickles, beans. You name it, she canned it.

On the top of each jar, she would write the date they had been preserved. Every once in a while I would see her look at a date and say, "Oh my, these have been here for a while. I hope they are still good." Sometimes the food was five, six, or seven years old! Whenever it came time to pop open one of those jars, they were *always* just as good as the day she put them in there.

The last two verses of Psalm 121 end with the subject of preservation:

[7] The LORD shall preserve thee from all evil: he shall preserve thy soul.

[8] The LORD shall preserve thy going out and thy coming in from this time forth, and even for evermore.

God *promises* that He "shall" preserve me. All I can take that to mean is this: that I will be properly protected – just like food properly preserved. I am in the palm of my Saviour's hand. God holds me closely and protectively. He assures me, "I'm not going to let anything happen to you that I don't want to happen to you."

The word "preserved" means *to keep alive; to keep in existence; to keep safe from harm or injury.*

We trust ourselves to keep food "alive." We trust ourselves to protect and preserve that food for years. How much more can God preserve and protect us? The preservation process is not new to Him.

Difficult times are not unique to us either. We can decide to stay with Christ during the difficult times, or we can choose to do our own thing. None of those who have chosen to stick with Christ regret it. However, those who have not stuck by Christ's side have many regrets.

It is important to remember that if we are children of God, our heavenly Father cares for us more than our natural father cares for his newborn child.

I think of my son, Mark, as he is entering into those formational stages. I could not picture *anybody* loving him more than Sarah and I love him. Sure, his schoolteachers may love him, but they are ready to give him back after school is over. Who can love a child like a mama? Who can love a child like a daddy? Yet, I am assured that our Father loves us more than any mama or daddy could love his own child. *That* is a lot of love.

Our Father also treats us and teaches us how a parent would treat his child. Sometimes true love involves hard-learned lessons. To the child, he cannot understand how hurt could ever be for his good, but the parent sees the bigger picture.

For instance, every once in a while there are certain things that I will let Mark do that he is not allowed to do.

I will tell him three or four times in the house, "Stop running in the house." I will warn him, but I will not stop him. I do not need to stand up and spank him yet, because all of a sudden you hear a "bam!" He will stand up and run crying to Sarah or me. We, as his parents, will take the time to patch up his mouth, check for any loose teeth, and Band-Aid up a finger. You can guess what we tell him before he leaves. "Now, Mark, that's why I told you not to run." How long does that instruction/warning last? It lasts until tomorrow comes around. When he gets home from school, he is high strung and ready to go. A conversation will occur something like this:

"Hey, Mark, remember what happened yesterday? What is on your finger right now?"

"A Band-Aid."

"Why is it there?"

"Because I ran yesterday."

29

"You want another one?"

"No."

That Band-Aid is a reminder of the wound he received from running. After looking at the Band-Aid and remembering the pain, he understands that running in the house is not worth it. Now, instead of running in the house, he *walks briskly* through the house!

God employs the same parenting tactic on us. No parent is going to let his child run into the street and be hit by a car to learn a lesson. God is the same way. Sometimes, though, God will allow us to "run in the house." Why? Because when I trip and fall flat on my face, He is there to bandage me up and dust me off.

Every once in a while, He causes us to reflect on our wounds. "Hey, remember the Band-Aid on your finger? Why do you have that?"

He loves me that much – teaching me how to grow and learn, even when it means allowing hurt in my life. When we experience hurt, it is a common reaction to blame God or to think that it is a sign that He loves me less. The difficult lesson proves that God is investing in His child's growth and maturity. It is the parenting sign of love.

That method of preservation makes little sense to children. I remember as a child how my dad would correct me. I remember telling myself that I would *never* say that to my child. Now that I am a parent myself, often I will correct one of my children and then think, "I can remember my dad saying the exact same thing!" The things I told myself I would never say were the very things my children needed to hear. I now know why my dad said certain things or why he did certain things. One day, my son will probably think the same thoughts.

Do you ever catch yourself thinking you know better than the Lord – our spiritual Parent? He knows how to preserve those He loves. Most of the time, we will not understand the reason for His process until we spiritually mature.

THE ULTIMATE MOTIVATION

J ESUS IS NOT JUST TALK. Everyone knows people who are all just talk. These types of people talk a good game, but when the rubber meets the road, that is all they are – talk, talk, talk.

I am glad that Jesus did not just talk about giving His life for us. He *did* give His life for us. He did not just *say* in Isaiah, "his name shall be called Wonderful, Counsellor, The mighty God, The everlasting Father, The Prince of Peace."[1] When the time came and when the timing was right, God said, "Jesus, it is time for you to go." Jesus did not randomly choose to step out of Heaven. He was ordered by His Father to do so. When God said, "Go." Jesus went. There was no question. At age 33, we find Him praying in the garden, requesting of His Father, "Lord, if it be thy will, let this cup pass from me."[2] It was not His Father's will, though. So,

---

[1] Isaiah 9:6b
[2] See Matthew 26:39

what did Jesus do? He "became obedient unto death, even the death of the cross."[3]

He went all the way for me.

How does God expect us to endure for Him? How can we be expected to make it through this quitting place when it seems so dark? When it seems no one understands? Look to Jesus as your *ultimate motivation.* Jesus did what He was expected to do, and the world is forever changed because of it. He understands the pain of your situation, and He invites you to take courage in His example. Make sure you are looking primarily to *Him* and not others.

People will fail you. I will fail you. There will be times when it seems like everyone is failing you. There will be times when you will fail yourself. There will be times when you will fail your children and when your children will fail you. You will fail your mate. Your mate will fail you. The list goes on, and on, and on. You will catch yourself thinking that the whole world and everyone in it is *all talk!*

That is why we are not commanded to look at each other. I am not just going to make it because you make it. You should not purpose in your heart to make it because I am making it. You and I should purpose in our hearts that we are going to make it *because Jesus made it.*

---

3 Philippians 2:8b

If Jesus would go through what He went through for me, why would I not go through what I am going through for Him?

When my eyes are lifted up on Him, I will not focus on all that is coming my direction. My eyes will not be on all the trials and all the health issues.

The minute we remove our eyes off the Lord, we become disoriented. We lose sight of the example He set. We forget what He endured with us in mind. We forget that this could be the day He comes again.

The Lord endured for me, and that is motivation enough not to quit. The Lord is coming for me, and that is inspiration enough to do something for Him.

PART

LISTENING TO SPIRITUAL PEOPLE

"Where no counsel is, the people fall: but in the multitude of counsellors there is safety." —PROVERBS 11:14

SAFETY IN COUNSEL

O NE THING I HAVE LEARNED through pastoring is that not many people like counseling...until they are in a lot of trouble. Then, when trouble comes, the counseling question they want answered is, "How do I get out of the trouble?" The hard truth is that they probably should have come to their pastor before they reached that point.

I want to be clear in that I believe the greatest counsel a person can receive is the counsel received from God's Word. Hearing from the Bible at Sunday School, Sunday morning, Sunday night, and Wednesday night is counsel. Open your heart to God's Word whenever it is preached. I promise you it will help you. However, I also believe we ought to receive counsel from godly people. As we dive into the second part of this book together, we will find that we can make it through the quitting places by listening to spiritual people who have already made it through difficult times.

Proverbs 11:14 says, "Where no counsel is, the people fall: but in the multitude of counsellors there is safety." A couple of chapters over in Proverbs 24:6, we find, "For by wise counsel thou shalt make thy war: and in multitude of counselors there is safety." There it is again. *Safety.* Two times in the same book, God promises that we can find safety in a multitude of counselors.

Let us not misinterpret those verses. Do not take them to mean that you should just ask ten people before you make every decision.

Just like the President of the United States has a cabinet of counselors, so should you. Your cabinet of counselors needs to be made up of spiritual people. One of your spiritual counselors should be your pastor. Another should be a godly deacon. Have a staff man and a wise layman on your cabinet, too.

Over the past nine years of my ministry, I have selected several pastors that I talk to and seek counsel from. One of those pastors has been pastoring for over 20 years. Another has pastored for 35. Another for almost 50. These are spiritual men. They have longevity in their ministries, and I enjoy listening to them.

Again, not all of your counselors have to be pastors. There are plenty of laymen in our church that I go to for counsel and advice on situations.

Are you always going to agree with your counselors? Probably not. Be very careful to listen, though, when the majority of them are saying the same thing.

For instance, say I have five counselors. Four of the five give me identical advice – counseling me to do the same exact thing. If, after hearing that godly counsel, I choose to do my own thing, I am probably going to find myself in a lot of heartache soon.

I have also found that the one counselor that did not have the same opinion as the other four just has a different viewpoint on the situation. That is understandable and to be expected. I am going to follow the four that agreed together. I have always found one thing in doing this. It is a Bible promise. You can already guess what it is.

Safety.

There have been many times I have prayed and prayed on a situation – looking to God alone the whole way through. There have been other times that I was helped by listening to spiritual people who had already made it through difficult times. *Everyone* that has ever gone through some difficult time can find comfort from those who have been through the same difficulties but are now on the victory side.

There is no greater joy that I experience than when a cancer patient comes up to me and says, "Let me tell you what God has taken me through." When they tell me their story, we start to rejoice together. Why does this sort of thing make people rejoice? Because God did not abandon us. You will find yourself rejoicing with them because they saw a victory, and they are giving you hope that you can have victory, too. Whatever the struggle, there is safety that can be had in spiritual counsel.

IDENTIFYING WITH OTHERS

THERE IS NO GREATER JOY as we go through a valley than to hear that somebody else understands exactly how we feel.

It is one thing when somebody says, "Well, I don't really know what you're going through, but let me give you some advice anyway." It is an entirely different experience when somebody says, "Oh, I have been there." When you hear something like that, your ears tend to perk up and you find yourself asking, "Really? How did you make it?"

From what I have found, those who have made it through the difficult times are not very eager to brag on themselves. They are not quick to walk around with their head held high, giving rapid-fire advice. They do not hand out business cards and tell people, "If anybody needs help in their marriage, come over here and see me. I can teach you a thing or two."

Now, the ones that have had struggles – maybe in marriage or maybe with a prodigal child – those parents are not the ones that are running around like they know it all. They had to learn some hard life lessons, and they are grateful to God that they made it through. Many times, I will call these types of people aside and ask, "I have a family going through a very similar situation that you faced. Could I send them to you?" So many people in our church have been used of God to help others because they made it through themselves.

Anyone who is going through a difficult time can find comfort from those who have faced similar situations but who are now on the victory side.

BATTLING FOR VICTORY

W E MUST ALSO REMEMBER that victory is only found on the other side of a battle. If you are looking for a victory, it is probably because you are in the midst of a battle right now. This is not a time to quit.

Could you imagine if all our soldiers who are currently deployed in Iraq one day decided to sit down somewhere and say, "We're done. We've had enough."? Deciding to stop fighting is not an option for a soldier.

As you read through Scripture, you do not find the children of God – some on horses, some on chariots, all with swords drawn – deciding to quit in the heat of the battle. I do not find any "we're done" moments in the book of Joshua. I do not see any examples of David's men abandoning a battle – leaving all their comrades in arms. The examples we are given did not act that way.

Why is it any different from the battles we face spiritually? Are not those stories meant as spiritual examples for us today?

Some of us catch ourselves in the heat of the battle saying, "You know what? I'm *done*." We wave the white flag of surrender and believe that we can walk away from the battle. The truth is that you *can* walk away from the battle anytime you want. However, nobody has ever walked away from a battle without *regret*.

Perhaps you walked away from a battle. You did not weather the quitting place. Several months later, you decided to pick up the sword and fight for the cause of Christ again. If so, you discovered a little secret: *the battle did not stop because you gave up*. You have to start right where you left off.

If someone told you that the Christian life was a bed of roses, that same someone sold you a bill of goods. You will never hear this author selling you that story. Why? Life is not going to be easy. Life has its challenges around every turn, around every corner. It seems like the challenges just keep coming and coming, and they come the most when we are at our weakest points. It is in these moments that we must remind ourselves that we are only going to experience victory on the other side of the battle.

MOUNTAINTOPS AND VALLEYS

Y OU MIGHT FIND YOURSELF SAYING in your heart, "I wish I could get to the mountaintop." We need to have a proper perspective about these mountaintop experiences. You cannot have a mountaintop *without having two valleys on either side.*

The majority of your life is going to be spent in the valley. That is not a doom-and-gloom philosophy – it is simply because for every one mountain, there are two valleys. The mountaintop experiences do come, but they are few and far between. They are moments of complete refreshment, of different perspective, and of absolute joy. When we journey past the mountaintop, we are going to find ourselves in the valley again. That is just the nature of traveling.

You will never find true growth on a mountaintop. True growth comes in a valley.

On a mountaintop, the air is thinner. It is harder to breathe. When you attempt to camp out up on the mountaintop, do not get disappointed when the wind blows you off the peak and you end up in the valley. That is life.

I have been given opportunities in the valleys of life that I would have never experienced on the mountaintop. I cannot tell you how many times a neighbor of mine, or someone who is not necessarily a member of our church, will come up to me and say, "Pastor, can I talk to you?" They have heard that I pastor a church in town and that I am facing some health difficulties. That opens a door for an almost stranger to ask for help about a difficult time they are facing. I have stood outside my house, sometimes into the early evening, trying to listen to a problem or a concern. The one answer that I can be confident to tell every neighbor is, "Make sure you know Christ." I do not claim to have all the answers, but I know that I have had the opportunity to lead three of the neighbors around my house to the Lord because they approached me in my driveway (during a valley of mine), and asked, "We heard you are a pastor. Can we talk to you?"

One lady, who drives a little grey car through our street, will ask for counsel whenever she has a problem. I remember the first time she stopped me in my yard and asked if she could talk to me. She asked me, "Are you sure it is all right that we talk outside here? Is your wife going to think that something is up -

you talking to a lady outside?" I said, "I doubt it; but if she does, she'll come running. Don't worry."

As we stood outside under that light pole, she began talking to me about some issues she was facing. I looked at her and I called her by name, and I said, "Do you know Christ?" She told me, "I don't even know what that means." I grinned and said, "I didn't think so." Then, I was able to go through the Gospel with her. Some forty-five minutes went by as we talked. Before I left, she bowed her head, prayed, and asked Jesus Christ to save her.

She has never come to church. I hope she will some day, but she has never attended a service.

When she heard I was sick, she knocked on our door and said, "I heard Pastor was sick. Would you let him know I am praying for him?" I am glad my wife did not say, "What? You have never even been to our church! Don't you know God is not hearing your prayers?!" She graciously said, "Oh, thank you so much. I will let him know."

There have been times she has pulled over to the side of our house in her car – maybe when I was outside with the kids or coming home from an event. She will role down her window and ask, "Pastor, can I ask you a quick question?" She will ask me a question about a heartache that she is experiencing, and I always ask her, "You remember when you received Christ as your Saviour?" "Oh, yes," is always the reply, " I remember I asked Jesus in my heart right over there." I will say, "You know, here are some things I would do if I were in your situation." Then before she leaves, I will say, "You need to come and visit our church. This drive-by pastoring thing doesn't work too well for me."

It all started because we had a garage sale. My wife had a baker's rack she was selling. My neighbor came over and bought it. And guess who was deputized to carry it? That is right...me! After I dropped off the merchandise at her front door, that opened up the relationship we have today.

We all must understand that there are going to be valleys. Some of my greatest times in my life, some of my wife's and my greatest times in marriage, have come during the valleys. They have not all come on the high points – on the mountaintops.

Romans 8:6 says, "For to be carnally minded is death; but to be spiritually minded is life and peace." The verse above informs us that we should be spiritually minded because if I am carnally minded, it is *death* to me spiritually. *I do not want to reason through spiritual things with a carnal mind.* Yet, that is the tendency.

Some who are saved and going through valleys experience spiritual dearth. Our walk with God is starving. Soul winning is a thing of the past. We used to be faithful to so many different avenues in the areas of God. But no more. If you catch yourself in this state, your mind is probably becoming carnal. A carnal mind in a crucial valley is only going to make matters worse. A carnal mind might be the reason the valley *never* seems to end. A God-allowed valley is meant for spiritual adjustment, but you will not be able to make the adjustment needed unless you are spiritual and *not* carnal.

You might be facing difficult situations in life while you are spiritually anemic. You might be in a spiritual draught. You might be saying to yourself, "I just don't know what to do." *Go back to His Word.* Fill up on the water that is the Bible.

Get back to the point where you were feeling your spiritual healthiest. Purpose in your heart to get back to the point when you and God were close friends. It is a lot better than feeling separated from God.

Valleys are full of opportunities. Use them whenever possible to get closer to God and to help other people.

JUDGE ME!

WHEN I AM GOING through the quitting places of life, it is important that I go to those that are spiritually on topside. If I get to these types of people, they can help me judge the issues I am facing.

To understand the point here, let us begin with the teaching found in First Corinthians chapter two.

> I Corinthians 2:13: Which things also we speak, not in the words which man's wisdom teacheth, but which the Holy Ghost teacheth; comparing spiritual things with spiritual.
>
> [14] But the natural man receiveth not the things of the Spirit of God: for they are foolishness unto him: neither can he know them, because they are spiritually discerned.
>
> [15] But he that is spiritual judgeth all things, yet he himself is judged of no man.
>
> [16] For who hath known the mind of the Lord, that he may instruct him? But we have the mind of Christ.

Did you catch what that last verse said? We have the mind of *Christ*! That is the mind I want when I am going through some troubles and some heartaches. During those days, when I say, "I just don't understand." I want to be able to tap into that spiritual mind that has been afforded to me. I want to claim the mind of Christ – what better mind to have!

So, what is the advantage of having the mind of Christ during a quitting place? First of all, we know that Christ's mind was determined not to quit.

Christ made it all the way to the cross, and by the way, *onto* the cross. He made it into the grave and then out of the grave. *That* is the determination and mindset that is crucial for me to have.

Usually, because we tend to decline spiritually during a quitting place, we lack the mind of Christ. We settle for our own carnal thoughts. Because of this, we must get to those on topside (those who have the mind of Christ and are spiritual). If we do not have the mind of Christ, we *must* get to someone who does.

You hear the statement all the time by offended people: "Stop judging me!" Most of the time, their statement is a clear indication that they have something to be judged about!

The ability to judge is Biblical. It is a sign that a person is spiritual. Again, I Corinthians 2:15 says, "But he that is spiritual judgeth all things..." Maybe you have had someone tell you, "Oh, well you are a Baptist. You are all judgmental." Hopefully, they mean you are spiritual, because a spiritual man "judgeth all things." Judging, in this context, has nothing to do with condemning or belittling someone. It has everything to do with carefully discerning, evaluating, and examining.

I judge whom my kids can and cannot hang out with. I judge whom my wife and I will and will not spend time with. I judge every day. We all do, and we all ought to. Judging does not mean that you think you are better than someone else. It means you are exercising discernment.

This is the time – in a quitting place – to intentionally put yourself under careful examination, under spiritual evaluation, and under wise discernment. Why is this so needed? Probably because you are not in a state of mind where you can spiritually discern yourself. You need the help of someone who is spiritual.

There is safety in being judged by a spiritual man, because the spiritual man is not going to spout off. Sometimes a spiritual man will say, "You know what? I don't know what to tell you right now, but if you give me some time I will get back to you." Being a know-it-all does not make someone spiritual. Sometimes, the best advice someone can give is, "I don't know. If you give me some time I will try my best to find out for you; and if I can't, I will get you somebody who can."

The job of restoring one who is quitting during that quitting place is given to the spiritual – not the one who *thinks* he or she is spiritual or who is just trying to *act* spiritual. Galatians 1:6 says, "He that is spiritual, restore such a one…" The "one" is referencing the one who has fallen. This job is not entrusted to the one who acts spiritual. It is not talking to the one who merely thinks they are spiritual. It is talking to the one who *is* spiritual.

Spiritual people are oftentimes not the ones running around saying they are. They are not usually the loudest of the group. They are the ones with hearts that are breaking for the person that is hurt. When approached their response is, "If I can help, I will help. I will do whatever I can."

With all your getting, get judgment…from a spiritual person.

THE HEART OF GOD

M AYBE THIS BOOK has found its way into the hands of someone who is not thinking of quitting on God. However, you are considering quitting on the *things* of God.

Maybe you are thinking of quitting on a marriage. Maybe you are considering to quit teaching your Sunday School class. Maybe you are thinking about taking a break from church. Maybe you are going to quit tithing, or driving a bus, or attending church altogether.

Let me say to you that quitting is not the heart of God.

All through the Scriptures, you will never find that God quit. From Genesis 1:1 all the way to the last verse in Revelation, you will never find a quitting Saviour. His people do, but our God does not.

Let me plead with you – from the heart of God – do not quit.

WHAT QUITTING TELLS GOD

NOBODY IS EXEMPT from going through difficult times. It is difficult times that make us depend on God more. Difficulties now strengthen us for the battles ahead. It is the preparation time that makes us who we need to be for the *most* difficult battle that we will face someday.

I do not know what your most difficult battle will be. For me, the most difficult battle may not be cancer. For me, the most difficult battle may not be with the pain in my leg. The most difficult thing may come twenty years from now. It might come by way of a heartache that one of my children will suffer with. It could be that in the future, my wife will be struggling. I do not know, but I want to show God that I can depend on Him *right now*. If this is the most difficult challenge that I ever struggle with, I pray that God finds me faithful.

If this is the most difficult thing that *you* ever struggle with (and it might be), stay faithful. If you quit now, it is not going to get easier.

Our church recently commissioned and sent a family to Tanzania, Africa to start a Christian orphanage – The Calvary's Love Children's Home. The Kessel family took an enormous step of faith, and I could not be more thrilled. I told our staff recently, "God is going to continue to take our church through moments of faith. We are asking a family to live by faith in Africa. If we are going to ask them to live by faith, God is going to put this church in a position where we are going to live by faith."

Faith has led me every step of the way – from the moment I started the ministry twelve years ago, to candidating at Calvary, and so on. I remind myself that God did not take us this far to abandon us now. Wherever you find yourself, God has not brought you this far on faith to abandon you either.

To quit on God is to say that He does not have what it takes to get you through the difficult times that you are facing. Romans 14:22-23 states, "Hast thou faith? have it to thyself before God. Happy is he that condemneth not himself in that thing which he alloweth. And he that doubteth is damned if he eat, because he eateth not of faith: for whatsoever is not of faith is sin."

How is your faith? We live in such a time of doubting Thomases. "I'll believe it when I see it," is the prevailing attitude. Real faith is believing it far before you ever see it.

That is why the Kessels went to Africa before we had all the money raised. That is why we keep the buses running. Faith is the church's mode of ministry. We *must* have faith. It prepares us for bigger challenges in the days ahead.

If you must see it before you believe it, you *will* quit. If we do not continue in faith, we are telling God that *He did not have what it takes to get us through*. We all know that is not the case.

BEWARE OF BITTER FINGER POINTING

THOSE WHO HAVE STAYED FAITHFUL to Christ and have made it through the quitting places are often more happy and humble than those who have quit on God. Many people that I run into who have quit on God have a definite arrogance about them. They can rattle off a list of reasons as to why they quit and why they are justified in doing so. They begin to blame so and so and such and such. I will run into them years later, and they are still repeating the same story…like a broken record.

Then, there are those who I run into who did not quit on God. They have such a happiness and humility about them. They will say, "I almost quit, but I am so happy I didn't."

There are times when difficulties might be the chastening of God. This is not always the case. However, it is between the believer and God to determine. It is for this reason that we must be very careful about whom we are pointing our accusatory finger at. We are quick to blame circumstances, people, and even God for our troubles. We are *slow* to indict ourselves.

Job 5:17 tells us, "Behold, happy is the man whom God correcteth: therefore despise not thou the chastening of the Almighty:" If you are honest with yourself and you realize that this "trial" is actually God-sent punishment brought on by your own sin, there is only one action you should do. You must *embrace* God's chastening hand.

No one is overflowing with joy as they are getting spanked. You can accept it, though. You can learn from it and allow it to make you better. You can get right with God as a result of it.

Understand that God does not want to spank you – just as any sane parent does not want to spank their child. God has a parent's heart toward His children.

Sometimes a quitting place is brought on because the person involved has abandoned the basic principles of God's Word. As a result, God loves us enough to help us get back to where we ought to be. Proverbs 3:11 gives us this advice, "My son, despise not the chastening of the LORD; neither be weary of his correction:" Also, Hebrews 12:6 says, "For whom the Lord loveth he chasteneth..." God loves us so much that He will keep us on the straight and narrow if we let Him. He will help us.

It is easy for pride to well up in hearts during these moments. Human nature does not want to admit that *I* am the problem. Instead, if something is going wrong, *surely* it must be someone or something else's fault.

Quitting places are sometimes spankings, and spankings are always building times in our life.

DEPENDING ON A PROMISE

W HEN YOU FIND YOURSELF in a quitting place, remember that God promised to never abandon those that are saved.

As a final thought for this section on listening to spiritual people, I want to leave you with the promise in Hebrews 13:5: "Let your conversation be without covetousness; and be content with such things as ye have: for he hath said, I will never leave thee, nor forsake thee."

Depend on the promise of God that He will *never* leave you or forsake you. If you cannot depend on this promise, all the counsel and spiritual guidance in the world will not help. Know that you do not have to face your world alone.

PART

LETTING ANYTHING GO THAT COULD HINDER GROWTH

"But none of these things move me, neither count I my life dear unto myself, so that I might finish my course with joy..."—ACTS 20:24a

WE ALL HAVE A PAST

I BELIEVE THAT THE DEVIL is in the middle of his final attack on the children of God. He is out to ruin homes and hurt families. He knows that the strength of the church of God is in the families within it.

So many of these families are made up of broken homes. It is wonderful to see how God takes broken homes and begins the reconstruction process! The true strength of the church is not *just* the families that are in it. True strength is measured by the amount of time that those families are walking with God and yielded to God.

The devil does not like this whole revival process. He is bent on *reminding us of our past* and therefore crippling our future. The devil knows that if you are living in the past, then you have no future.

The Apostle Paul personally knew what it was to have a past. If anyone had "reason" to think he could not be used for God, it was Paul. Yet, he writes in Philippians 3:12-14:

[12] Not as though I had already attained, either were already perfect: but I follow after, if that I may apprehend that for which also I am apprehended of Christ Jesus.

[13] Brethren, I count not myself to have apprehended: but this one thing I do, *forgetting those things which are behind, and reaching forth unto those things which are before,*

[14] I press toward the mark for the prize of the high calling of God in Christ Jesus.

[15] Let us therefore, as many as be perfect, be thus minded: and if in any thing ye be otherwise minded, God shall reveal even this unto you. (Emphasis added)

The verse I have picked as my life's verse (Acts 20:24) goes right along with this thought, "But none of these things move me, neither count I my life dear unto myself, so that I might finish my course with joy, and the ministry, which I have received of the Lord Jesus, to testify the gospel of the grace of God."

A well-rounded church did not arrive at that position because its pastor had all the answers. The only way a church becomes well rounded, balanced, and able to make it through the quitting places is if the church has its eyes on Christ. Note that when you have your eyes on Christ, your eyes are not *on your past!*

We *all* have a past, and the devil tries to remind each and every one of us about it. He tries to beat you up. He bullies you.

Sometimes, he will remind you by bringing somebody back from your past. It was just last week that I talked on the phone to a man from our area. He said, "You won't believe what happened. I haven't seen this old friend of mine in 25 years. I have had victory over this area of my life. All of a sudden, this person from my past reappears. In front of my teenager, who I am trying to rear for the Lord, he says, 'You remember the days when we used to go out and do such and such?' That was 25 years ago!" He told me he had to take his teenager aside to do some explaining.

Why would something like that happen? The devil wanted to remind him of his past. He does the same to you and me. Is that not true?

The devil tricks you into doing something and then blames you for it after you do it.

There is pleasure in sin for a season. The Bible specifically says so.[4] Many have experienced that pleasure. After the season comes to an end, however,

---

[4] See Hebrews 11:25

nothing but heartache follows. Devastation comes. Maybe you have been there.

You will be reminded of that devastation by the devil himself over and over and over again. The devil knows that regret is effective in making you feel like you are not worthy of accomplishing something for God. He knows that you will look back in the years to come and wish you never had experienced the pleasure. The pleasure is not worth the price that you are paying now.

As a pastor, I have counseled for some time now. During some of these appointments, I try to understand what the problem is. We have to dig a little deeper and discuss the past. Sometimes, as we unearth something that has never been dealt with, the tears begin to flow. It is almost like grabbing a water spigot – the more you turn, the more of the past begins to flow out.

So many have tried to bury their sinful past, because they are ashamed of it, instead of dealing with their sin. Nothing is hid from the Lord, and He wants us to be honest with Him about our past.

Claim 1 John 1:9, which says, "If we confess our sins, he is faithful and just to forgive us our sins, and to cleanse us from all unrighteousness." That is a verse to the saved.

So, do not try to hide your sin. Confess it, and remind yourself of God's promise that He will forgive us. Do not act as though you are innocent of the crime. Admit it, confess it, get right with God, and move on with life.

If your sin requires you to go to a brother or a sister in Christ, then go to them and get the issue right. It is far easier to get right with someone than to cover, to hide, or to run. It is much more devastating if God has to reveal a hidden sin than if we would have been honest.

It is hard to imagine Paul completely forgetting his past, as if it was washed away from his memory through amnesia. He had a lot of memories that I am sure the devil would bring up as he sat there in a prison cell. I am sure the devil visited him a time or two and brought back flashbacks of the Christians Paul had martyred. However, Paul was greatly used of God *despite his past*. A big reason is that Paul fully admitted his past, fully confessed his past, and fully pursued his future. Paul had to say, "forgetting those things which are behind," "reaching forth unto those things which are before," and "I press toward the mark."

The past is exactly that – *the past*. Be careful on those weak days, those quitting places. Be careful not to give the devil an opportunity to come and steal your joy. Joy is a choice. Joy is *your* choice.

Confessing When Convicted

S OMEONE ONCE SAID, "The past is history. The future is a mystery. Today is a gift, and that's why it's called the present." If you are still breathing air, you have a *gift*, an opportunity, to get right with God.

It could be that you have never put your faith in Christ as your Saviour. Maybe you are procrastinating – living as though you are guaranteed tomorrow.

Maybe that rich man[5] thought he had more time, but now he is in Hell. He is lifting up his eyes, hoping for another chance yet knowing his chances have been used up. He does not see Abraham afar off any longer. He is in torment.

It could be that you are saved, but there is something between your soul and your Saviour – unconfessed sin. Maybe you, too, are living as though you are guaranteed tomorrow.

---

[5] See Luke 16

The fact of the matter is that we are not guaranteed another second here on Earth. The signs of the times are not just found in the book of Revelation. You can see them taking place as you watch the news broadcast before you go to bed. The thought that Christ could come at any time should be reason enough to be constantly right with God.

The Holy Spirit will convict and convict and convict you of your unconfessed sin. But as soon as we truly claim 1 John 1:9, He will never bring the past of the saved up again...*here on Earth*.

I tagged those last three words "here on Earth" to the above sentence for a reason. Yes, I believe that God will wash our sins away and that He will remove them as far as the east is from the west. However, I also believe that it will be revealed to us why we did not receive certain rewards.

First Corinthians chapter three has much to say about how our works will be tried to see what sort they were. Some works that we did will appear as gold, silver, and precious stones (works that mattered for God). Others will be represented as wood, hay, and stubble (works that were vain, empty, worthless). There will be a "trial by fire" to see which works remain and which ones are consumed. I think we will know which works for God were done in the flesh and which ones were done in the Spirit.

I do not wish to give the false hope that unconfessed sin goes unnoticed when you get to Heaven. God knows which deeds were done for His glory and which were done for your own. It is *impossible* to do good deeds for God with unconfessed sin on your heart. You can look the part and play the part, but God knows the heart. It is true that He has forgiven you of your sin, but He is definitely not going to *reward* you for your sin.

That might be a different train of thought for some. Again, I know sins have been forgiven and sins have been forgotten. The fact, though, is that 1 John 1:9 is talking to the believer. He is faithful and just to forgive us (the saved) from all unrighteousness. This does not mean a person must get saved over and over again. It *does* mean that a child of God needs to get right over and over again – producing a good conscience toward and a good relationship with the Lord.

Many people are good at talking their way out of problems. They justify themselves so well to others. I wonder if we would have the arrogance to argue with God when our works are tried by fire? I do not think God is going to be very interested in our rebuttal.

I can imagine myself daring to say to God, "Hey, that's not right, God. That right there shouldn't have been burned up. Hold on now!" I think that if such a conversation ever took place, God would reply,

"Cameron, I'm never wrong. I wish you would have been right with me."

I have heard many people make arguments like, "You know what? God is all about love; and no matter what I do, when I get to Heaven, everything is going to be cool. He is not going to care what I did or didn't do." Might I remind you, if you are of that thought that there is a reason why God has to wipe our tears away.

It is just a thought. Unwrap the gift of the present, and clear the air between you and your Saviour today. You will be eternally glad that you did.

Refuge and Repentance

M ANY TIMES the past hurts before Christ will cause a believer to take certain steps of faith. As I have counseled members, I have given recommendations that they help out in a certain one of our church ministries. Sometimes I will get the reply, "Oh, Pastor, I couldn't do that. You just don't know my past." I will ask, "Aren't you saved?" They will say, "Well, yes. But Pastor, if anybody ever found out..." I will say, "If anybody ever found out and condemned you over it, they are not following the same God that I am following."

I am glad to say that we have people that serve the Lord who have a rough past.

Understand though, we are not foolish in our behavior either. We are not letting child molesters work with our children, etc. We are careful in all of those areas.

The fact, however, is that people do not have to be perfect to serve the Lord. Else, there would be no one serving Him! I have preached it from the day I became the pastor: the church should not be built in part on our ex-pastors, ex-deacons, ex-Sunday School teachers. The church is built on ex-drug addicts and ex-street walkers. It is partly built on those who were homeless at one time, whom Christ reestablished back in their community and into society again.

As I look at the faces of our members every service, I know I am looking at those who have found their "city of refuge" – the church house.

There was something special about the old Catholic churches in history. We are told that when people ran to the walls of a Catholic church, the law could not touch them as long as they were in its confines. They were safe and protected.

The priest could walk boldly out of the front of those doors to the lawmen and say, "This man has sanctuary. As long as he is within these walls, the matter is between him and God, not him and you."

Sanctuary! The church is our sanctuary.

According to our law, that word does not nearly have the meaning that it used to have. If you are running from the police and run into church, there is not much I can do. You can hold onto my hand and ask me to tell the policeman that he cannot touch you. I am just warning you – it is probably not going to do you much good. I can plead your case, but the policeman is probably going to say, "God bless you, Pastor. If you want to hold his hand in jail, you can definitely go with him!" The word "sanctuary" does not mean the same anymore.

Nonetheless, you can go all the way back to the Old Testament and read about the cities of refuge that were scattered all around. A person guilty of a crime could run as fast as he could to the nearest city of refuge. As long as he lived within the walls of that city, he could not be touched. *That* is what the church house ought to be. A city of refuge.

Church acts as a refuge for those who come with true repentance, not to those who want to play church. It will never feel like a city of refuge for the rebelious. It is to those who really want to do something for God in God's way. It is for those who come to God and say, "I am nothing, but I want You to make me something." Convicted of sin, that man turns from his ways (repents), and starts allowing God to use him.

That is why some with terribly rough pasts are able to come to church and feel safe, to feel free. You can be an usher, you can work on a bus route, you can sing in a choir, you can work in a Sunday School Class, you can run security, etc. etc.

Serving in the church is going to require some to stop walking around like the wounded victim that the world taught them they are. You are going to have to claim the promise that, "greater is he that is in you, than he that is in the world." (I John 4:4b)

We sing that song, "We are more than conquerors through Him who loves us so. The Christ who dwells within us is the greatest power we know." Some walk into the church house, and they have the gloom-and-doom attitude that says, "You just don't know what I have been through." God does. Through Him, you can smile again.

After you have proven to yourself, to God, and to others that your past is the past, you will start seeing God use your testimony. God can use the story of your past (your testimony) as an example of a transformed life in order to point others to Him.

In order to "jump in" with both feet, there are some past issues that we have to let go. You will never feel truly safe or accepted inside the city of refuge until you have let the past go. No Christian who is right with God will sift through your past and point out your mistakes. Your pastor will not. Christ will not. You should not either.

Get busy living and serving in your newfound refuge.

A DOUBLE-MINDED MAN

T HE DEVIL is constantly calling you back to the world. He tempts you with the memories of sinful pleasures you experienced long ago. The thought *scares* you. You live in fear – not that your past will catch up with you, but that you will fall back into sin.

If the devil is using your past as a vice around your neck, you need to learn to let it go. Second Timothy 1:7 states, "*For God hath not given us the spirit of fear*; but of power, and of love, and of a *sound mind.*" (Emphasis added) When I was saved, God did not fill my mind with fear. He gave me power, love, and a sound mind. Fear is not found in a sound mind.

The mind that I use to think nowadays is different than the mind that I had back in the world. It is a sounder mind. Why? Because I can get into the Bible, and I can seek the mind of Christ – purging any unstable thoughts.

The book of James tells us, "A double-minded man is unstable in all his ways." When you stop going soul winning, and you stop being faithful to church, and you stop smiling, and you stop seeking after the things of Christ, you begin slipping back to the way you used to be. You start finding joy in worldly friends and in past pleasures.

It is no wonder you are confused!

When the flesh wars against the Spirit and Spirit wars against the flesh, a double-minded man is the result. He will be unstable in all his ways. He is fearful.

You are tempted to quit on any number of things when you are double minded. You might be at a quitting place right now, and it may be due to the fact that you are holding onto and indulging in your past. Let it go. Sever the ties. Let the Holy Spirit continue His work in you.

The Holy Spirit begins to work in the heart of the saved by convicting their conscience. What a wonderful peace comes over an individual who will come back by way of repentance. Friend, come back to God and say, "Father, I know I have hurt you. I know I have hurt you deeply; but God, if you will forgive me, I promise I will try harder." You know what God will *always* say? "Sure. I forgive you."

Most people that slip back into the world never really repented in the first place. The "repentance" was nothing more than a fake apology. We think we can fool God like we do everyone else.

My kids do that sometimes. I will tell Mark, "Tell your sister you are sorry for throwing her doll down the stairs." Mark will tell his sister, "I'm sorry." Then, I will say, "Now, mean it." Then he will look at me like he has no idea what in the world that means – to "mean it." He will say again, "I'm sorry, Madeline." Well I know he does not quite mean it yet, but one day my kids are going to remember their daddy saying, "Say it and mean it."

As we get older, we know exactly what it means – to mean it. How many times have we said, "I'm sorry" to God or others, only hoping that it appeases them? God knows my heart more than I know my own heart.

Quit trying to hold onto your sinful past and your Christian future at the same time. God wants you to always have a sound mind, not a double mind.

Things are Never the Same

ONE OF THE SADDEST THINGS that I have watched people do these last nine years is this, they return to the past that God rescued them from. They make this decision thinking that things can be exactly as they used to be. Such is not the case.

I have seen many people get victory. Whether they were in a youth group twelve years ago or whether they were adults in church ten years ago, I have seen the whole process. I have observed folks do great for about six or seven years. Then all of a sudden, something overwhelms them. Before you know it, they are back to what they were doing before they got saved – thinking life can revert back with no problem.

I have counseled people who have told me a bit about their past, "Be careful, because the devil does not like how far you have come, and he will do everything he can to get you back to where you used to be. The devil wants to hurt the heart of God more than anything. He knows that the best way to hurt God is to hurt His children."

John chapter five deals with this idea of what happens when one attempts to go back to his past. Jesus had just healed a man by saying, "Take up thy bed and walk." Remember the story? The following verses tell us what happened right after that:

[10] The Jews therefore said unto him that was cured, It is the sabbath day: it is not lawful for thee to carry thy bed.

[11] He answered them, He that made me whole, the same said unto me, Take up thy bed, and walk.

[12] Then asked they him, What man is that which said unto thee, Take up thy bed, and walk?

[13] And he that was healed wist not who it was: for Jesus had conveyed himself away, a multitude being in that place.

[14] Afterward Jesus findeth him in the temple, and said unto him, *Behold, thou art made whole: sin no more, lest a worse thing come unto thee.* (Emphasis added)

You know what I have observed? It is never the same when a saved person goes back to the life that God saved him out of. Nothing is the same.

The booze does not hold the same appeal. Drugs and alcohol are not the same as they used to be before God saved them. It is worse. It is worse going back because the child of God knows better. James 4:17 says, "Therefore to him that knoweth to do good, and doeth it not, to him it is sin." The backslider finds himself as a saved individual trying to live a sinner's life. He is not going to be able to live it. He is going to be constantly convicted of sin.

As a matter of fact, that is why a lot of Christian men and women who have gone back and thrown their lives away have a lot of anger issues today. Many are depressed. Some are suicidal. That which God saved them from has now become worse than it used to be. The joy that they thought they could get a hold of from the bottle cannot be found. They are unable to drown all their sorrows away. *The Holy Spirit can even be heard through a drunken state.* The saved individual has a hard time quenching that Spirit entirely, even when he is backslidden.

This backsliding action on the believer's part shows that they did not sever all ties that bound them from the past they came from. One does not return to the world unless he has been thinking about doing so for some time. No Christian suddenly decides to walk back into sin. Sin starts as a small seed thought in the mind before it ever settles in the heart.

Let me ask you, "Reader, how is your mind right now?" Maybe you are running back to your old ways and the devil has control of your thoughts. It could be that you have not severed all the ties of the past, even though you have convinced everyone that you have.

My wife and I do not run with people outside of our church. There is a reason for that. We have neighbors that will often invite us over for barbeques during the summer. I will say something like, "Oh sorry, I don't think that will work." Slowly, but surely, after asking us several times, they start to get the point. We will still be very friendly, but they will stop inviting us over.

A little boy in the neighborhood came running up to me and said, "It would be great if your son could come over and play with me." Well, I did not feel like bursting his bubble right then. It was not the time or the place. I simply said, "You know, you give me time to think on that and we will talk later." Why would I do something like that? I knew what the home was like over there, and I knew it would not be good for my son to be exposed to it.

We are still on extremely good terms with our neighbors. We came home from church this past Sunday and our trash was already taken out. I asked my wife, "Honey, did you take out our trash?" It turns out that our neighbor has been trying to help us for weeks during my health difficulties, and he decided to take our trash out for us. He is one of the kindest men I know. I have witnessed to him on several occasions. Unfortunately, he always has a nice excuse for me not to go further into the Gospel with him. I am confident he is going to let me take him there eventually. We invite him to church all the time. I cannot wait for the day when he comes to visit.

Though Christians should sever the ties of the past (and to things that remind us of the past), it does not mean that I cannot reach the world like God commanded me too. I am stronger in reaching the world when I have severed all the ties of the past that bind me to the things of Satan.

Trying to move forward for God while tied to the past is like trying to drive a boat that is tied to the pier.

WEEDS IN THE GARDEN

I F YOU HAVE A GARDEN, it is essential that you keep it weeded. Weeds will keep those tomatoes from looking good, from growing well, from developing properly. Weeds will hurt the squash. Weeds will hurt anything that you are trying to grow.

Weeds may look pretty for a while. Some even resemble flowers. That is, when they are small.

When they start getting bigger and bigger, that which looked pretty at first begins to overrun what you are trying to grow.

If you do not keep a close eye on your garden, you will have to untangle weeds out of this bush here and from around that plant over there. Every time you pull, you end up damaging some of the good leaves and some of the good plants. You lose some of what you were trying to grow. You subtract from its beauty.

You did not rip out the weeds when they were small.

If you wait too long before trying to correct some "small" sinful tendencies, you are going to lose your beauty. Your countenance is going to fall. You are going to lose your joy. You waited too long.

It is never an enjoyable experience pulling up weeds. Yet it is much easier to do so when you first begin to see a sinful habit form, rather than when you realize the weed is ruining your life.

God has given us gardening instructions on growing our life properly. He says in II Peter 3:18, "But grow in grace, and in the knowledge of our Lord and Saviour Jesus Christ." Notice He did not say to grow in your knowledge of Pawn Stars, Hawaii Five-0, The Voice, or America's Got Talent. Some are *very* knowledgeable about television and not so knowledgeable about our Lord.

When you are walking with the Lord and spending time in His Word, you start looking at your life more closely. You spot weeds quicker. You find yourself desiring to please the Lord in all things in your well-kept garden of grace.

RELIEF OR REGRET

H OW ARE WE GOING to make it through the quitting places? We have seen that we are going to have to let some things go that are hindering our growth. Let me leave you with a final thought for this section.

There is nothing worse than the following type of doctor's visit that I have experienced: First, they make me put on an embarrassing hospital gown. Then, they make me stand up. The doctors measure both of my legs, and then they say I can sit back down and wait. They go out of the room and talk for ten or fifteen minutes. When they return, they say, "We don't have any idea what is wrong. We don't have a clue."

There is nothing worse than that.

There is nothing more joyful, however, when the opposite of that visit occurs. When doctors have told me for so long that they do not have a clue about my health, they enter the room and say, "You know what? We found it. We know exactly what your problem is."

It is a feeling of absolute relief. I can sit there and say, "Wow! Praise the Lord."

Often, we cannot predetermine when those times of relief happen. That is in God's hands. Most of this book is dedicated to those who are facing a quitting place because of situations *far* outside their control.

This section, however, deals with an area that is totally in *your* control. You might be facing a quitting place right now because your sinful past is now becoming your present. There is something between your soul and your Saviour. You have one hand on the world and another barely hanging onto God. There are weeds in your garden.

There is nothing worse than when you sit in church, knowing you are supposed to get something right. Yet, you resist. You find that the walk back to your car is a long walk. You ask yourself, "Why didn't I go to the altar?"

There is nothing more joyful, however, than when you stand up from the altar and you have actually got some things right with God. The drive home could not be sweeter. Your pillow that night could not be softer.

Do not allow yourself to end life with regret. Let go of whatever is hindering your spiritual growth.

PART

LEARNING WHAT YOU CAN

"A wise man will hear, and will increase learning; and a man of understanding shall attain unto wise counsels:"
—*PROVERBS 1:5*

BACK TO SCHOOL

A S A CHILD, I never wanted to sit in the front row of my Sunday School classroom. The teacher would often call on some of the students to stand in front of the class and write an answer on the chalkboard. I enjoyed Sunday School, but definitely did not want to be called on. So, I made it a point to sit in the back. I enjoyed the comfort of knowing that if I sat in the back, the chances of being called on were slim.

Throughout my life, there have been many times where I felt as though the Lord called me all the way to the front of the class and was requiring me to write my answer on the chalkboard. Have you ever felt that way? Have you ever wanted to sit in comfort and let someone else stand in front of everyone else?

I watched this phenomenon take place in the early years of our Christian school. I was teaching some of our school classes back then – one of those classes being Math. I would write the problem on the chalkboard and then ask one of the students to come up in front of the class. There would always be one student solving the problem on the board while the rest of the class was solving it in their books. Out of the whole class, the one student who wanted to get the answer right more than *anyone* else was the student at the chalkboard. Why would that student be afraid of getting the answer wrong? Because everyone is watching. Because failing the test would be embarrassing.

Every once in a while in life we feel like we are standing in front of the class and everyone else is sitting. All eyes are on us. People are taking notes on how we face the problem. We tell ourselves, "Everybody is staring at me. Everybody is watching me."

God will call our name. He will make it so other people can see us – right in front of the class. He puts His arm around us and says, "I need people to see that you can make it through this problem because this is the only way I can also teach others."

We have to learn this way sometimes, and learning is not always easy.

Somebody once said, "Don't get mad when God is silent through the hardest test of life. The teacher never talks when it is time for the student to take a test. The teacher is always silent."

Does that mean God leaves us during our most challenging times? No. It means He is standing by our side, watching us. He wants to see what step we are going to take next – wondering if we have been listening to His previous instructions before test day.

WISE STUDENT, FOOLISH STUDENT

N O STUDENT CHOOSES the test he takes. That is not in his control. We do, however, have control over our actions and attitudes when God chooses to "take us to school." We can respond wisely or foolishly.

Our desire ought to be like the wise man of Proverbs 1:5: "A wise man will hear, and will increase learning; and a man of understanding shall attain unto wise counsels:" In contrast to increasing learning, the fool will *not* learn the valuable lessons that he is supposed to learn. The foolish student ends up failing the class and having to repeat the course.

Have you ever failed a class in college? The college student looks at his report card and says, "What?!" The immediate reaction is to blame whom? The *teacher*.

The college student looks at his report card and makes an excuse: "I am pretty sure the teacher did not even cover this. Though I am only one of two who failed in a class of 25, it is definitely the teacher's fault."

Usually, the two people who failed were the ones who sat by each other, talking through all of the lectures. You cannot justly blame the teacher for your failing grade if you were not paying attention to what he was teaching during class.

Be careful with whom you go through the quitting places. Make sure you are going through this school of testing with people who have a track record of victory.

Right now, the senior saints in our church are some of my most favorite people to hang out with. They cannot walk faster than I can! They know what it is like to spend some time in a wheelchair. They understand what heartaches are. When I talk with them, they rarely discourage me.

I do not like defeatist attitudes. I do not like when people see me lying in the hospital bed and say, "Oh, you look terrible." I want to respond, "Thanks. You look great, too." If you are down, discouraged, and in the hospital, more discouragement is not ever going to help. Those who have been through it themselves are very slow to tell you how badly you look. They are slow to say anything at all, really.

I find that the more God takes me through, the less I want to tell people why they are going through what they are going through. I am slow to spell out remedies to anybody, since I know how much I do not like it when people spell out remedies to me: "Well, let me tell you what might help your cancer. If you drink 5,000 gallons of carrot juice, you will turn orange; but it may help with cancer."

Those who have never been through it themselves are so quick to rattle off remedies. Those that have been through a quitting place are very slow in that regard. Those who have been through it understand that there is an opportunity to get some helpful advice. However, advice cannot be forced onto anyone. A person is only ready when they are ready. When they are ready, they will ask.

As I go through the quitting places, I want to make sure that I am learning what I can. I want to be wise *with whom* I receive counsel, *when* I receive counsel, and *how* I receive counsel.

This first chapter of Proverbs has much to say about fools and foolish decisions. Proverbs 1:7 tells us, "The fear of the LORD *is* the beginning of knowledge: *but* fools despise wisdom and instruction." Verse 22 of the same chapter says, "How long, ye simple ones, will ye love simplicity? and the scorners delight in their scorning, and fools hate knowledge?" Verse 32, "For the turning away of the simple shall slay them, and the prosperity of fools shall destroy them."

Nobody wants to be a fool. Nobody delights in taking a test for which he is not prepared. The type of student we chose to be is entirely our choice. Wise students pass the tests. They make it through the quitting places. Fools do not pass the tests, and they usually blame the teacher.

Our Teacher requests that we learn from Him. He informs us, "I was in all points tempted like as you are, yet without sin."6 He has something to teach us if only we will listen.

We read in the beginning of this section that "a wise man will hear." I ask you, dear Reader, are you hearing the Teacher? Are those you are seated next to helping you or hindering you?

---

6 See Hebrews 4:15

REPEATING THE GRADE

I T IS NOT FUN to hear that you failed. It is not fun to be a seventh grader twice. Anyone who has ever had to be held back a grade in school due to the lack of academic performance knows what it is like to have to redo the grade. When all of your classmates are advancing to the eleventh grade and you are not, it is difficult to think of a cool-sounding explanation: "Well, I really enjoyed the tenth grade. I just wanted to try it twice." Let me tell you, repeating a grade is not all that cool...so learn the first time.

Someone once said that the Bible as an acrostic (B-I-B-L-E) stands for *basic instruction before leaving earth.* If the Bible has something to teach me as I am going through a quitting place, I want to learn what I need to the first time. I *definitely* do not want to have to repeat the grade.

The Bible tells us plainly in Romans 15:4 that the Bible was written so that we could learn: "For whatsoever things were written aforetime were written for our learning, that we through patience in comfort of the scriptures might have hope." Why would I need the Scriptures to comfort me unless it was for a difficult time?

It has been said about the Book of Psalms that each psalm is like a little hug from God. After reading a psalm, it is as though God wraps His arms around us, squeezes us close, and says, "Hey, I want to remind you that I am here."

God never promised that the Christian life would be like a bed of roses. It is great to know, though, that He promised to never leave us nor forsake us. If you thought that getting saved would make all of your problems go away, you thought wrong. After you get saved, it seems like problems are dumped on you by the truckload. Problems happen to the saved and the unsaved. The unbelievable benefit to the saved, however, is that with spiritual eyes we can feel the comfort of God through the pages of His Word.

How does God teach us? By what method does He make us better people? Many times, He wounds us. He loads us with a burden.

Why would the loving Father do this to His children? Why does He allow some of us to be flat on our backs? Why is the burden so heavy that we are forced to fall beneath the weight to our knees?

The answer: You cannot help but look God square in the face when you are lying on your back. You cannot help but pray when you fall to your knees.

You want to learn the lesson God is trying to teach you *the first time.* Maybe the goal is for you to develop a deeper appreciation for His Word. Maybe the goal is for you to discover His presence through prayer. Whatever the case and for whatever the reason, discover what God is teaching you.

TAUGHT THE HARD WAY

T HE DIFFICULT TIMES in our life are to be accepted as times of learning. King Nebuchadnezzar in Daniel chapter four could Amen this point better than any. After being taught the hard way by God, the king has this to say about the experience:

> Daniel 4:34 And at the end of the days I Nebuchadnezzar lifted up mine eyes unto heaven, and mine understanding returned unto me, and I blessed the most High, and I praised and honoured him that liveth for ever, whose dominion is an everlasting dominion, and his kingdom is from generation to generation:
>
> [35] And all the inhabitants of the earth are reputed as nothing: and he doeth according to his will in the army of heaven, and among the

inhabitants of the earth: and none can stay his hand, or say unto him, What doest thou?

[36] At the same time my reason returned unto me; and for the glory of my kingdom, mine honour and brightness returned unto me; and my counsellors and my lords sought unto me; and I was established in my kingdom, and excellent majesty was added unto me.

[37] Now I Nebuchadnezzar praise and extol and honour the King of heaven, all whose works are truth, and his ways judgment: and those that walk in pride he is able to abase.

This is after seven years of King Nebuchadnezzar acting like an animal out in the field. He was dethroned by God and given the mind of a wild animal. His hair became like eagle's feathers. His fingernails and toenails grew like talons. He would graze the fields like a cow.

Then the Bible tells us that his reason returned to him. After those seven long years...*he learned*.

He had to learn the hard way. In his case, he had to learn the hard way because he would not listen to the man of God. There are many reasons why God chooses to resort to teaching someone the hard way.

If you find yourself having to be taught the hard way, there is a correct way you should react. Go to God in prayer and say, "Show me, dear Lord, what You are trying to teach me. Here I am. I know You will never give me more than I can handle. I am not going to quit on You. Instead, I am going to depend on You to see me through. I am not going to walk around with a sour face or a scowl. I am not going to have a bad attitude and be grumpy toward everybody. Please give me the joy of the Lord. Let that joy be my strength like You promise. Please help me to learn what I need to learn through this."

THE DEMAND OF OBEDIENCE

T HERE WILL BE MANY TIMES that the Lord will try and get us to learn from the wisdom of His Word and the preaching or teaching of His man. These are the means of His instruction to us. He expects us to listen to Him through whatever means he chooses.

The children of God experienced their first defeat at Ai in the book of Joshua. Thirty-seven men of Israel died in the battle. The bloodshed of God's people could have been avoided if everyone would have listened to God's man, Joshua. We find that the man who did not listen was Achan.

Joshua 7:1 says, "But the children of Israel committed a trespass in the accursed thing for Achan, the son of Carmi, the son of Zabdi, the son of Zerah, of the tribe of Judah, took of the accursed thing: and the

106

anger of the Lord was kindled against the children of Israel."

In chapter six of Joshua (the previous chapter), Joshua takes the time to specifically warn the people, "Hey, I want to tell you that when we get to Jericho, everything belongs to God. We are to take *nothing*. Do not take of the accursed thing. Anything you take is cursed to you, but it is blessed if you give it to God."7

I can picture Achan as he comes across some of these precious spoils of war. He looks around to see if anybody is watching. He hides it all, but God saw where he hid it. He is confident that nobody knows, but God knew.

Achan was successful in hiding sin from Joshua. Achan was successful in hiding sin from all of Israel. Achan failed, though, when he tried to hide his sin from *God*.

The people returned from battle in defeat, shaking their heads. "Why did God let us down?" they must have wondered.

Then God revealed to Joshua that sin was in the camp. God has Joshua call all of the tribes of Israel. God points out the specific tribe. Then, the specific household. Then, the specific family. Then, specifically, Achan.

---

7 Author's paraphrase of Joshua 6:18-19

Achan and his whole family were stoned with rocks. All of their belongings burned. Why? God expects us to listen to His instructions. God gives blessings to His children who obey and punishment to those who do not obey.

Growing up, my mom would tell me, "Go clean your room." She expected it to be done. There were times when she would check to make sure we had done what she asked – sometimes at 10 o'clock at night before she went to bed. She sometimes discovered that we had stuffed everything under the bed instead of putting it all away. I remember her reaching under our beds, pulling out all the stuff, and piling it in the middle of the floor. She would then wake me up and make me clean the room (apparently not too concerned about me getting a good night's rest or that I had to go to school the next day). All she cared about was that I had disobeyed.

I would be overwhelmed by a pile the height of Mount Everest in the middle of my bedroom – waiting for me to get to the bottom of it! On top of that, she would come with a vacuum cleaner. That is the last sound a child wants to hear when he is trying to sleep. The sound of a vacuum cleaner late at night is still a sound that haunts me. I hated that vacuum!

I remember at other times disobeying and warranting a spanking from my parents. Seeing a sibling being spanked or receiving the spanking yourself is incentive enough to listen to the authority. If I listen, I see my parents smile. If I disobey, I see my parent's rod.

Think of what would have happened had Korah listened to Moses. The reason the ground swallowed up Korah was not because he had a disagreement with the man of God (Moses). It was because Korah was leading a rebellion against the man of God. All of a sudden, God made it very clear that the people were to heed the Word of God through Moses.

I guarantee that after that happened, everyone who was left behind was ready to do absolutely anything Moses said. Moses could have probably asked them to do anything he wanted. He did not abuse his power, though. Instead, he simply led the people on as God wanted. His strong desire was for the people to obey God, not him.

There will be many times that the Lord will try to teach us the wisdom of His Word through the preaching or teaching of his man, whoever that man may be. Achan could have lived a great life with his family if he would have listened. Korah could have been spared a whole lot of heartache had he submitted. Our heavenly Father has a "rod" that He will use if we do not listen and obey.

Go for the blessings of God by listening. Spare yourself the pain that comes from disobeying.

BEYOND OUR CONTROL

T HERE ARE TIMES in our lives where we know better, yet we still find ourselves doing what we know we should not do. These actions often have their own lessons, and we often learn them through deepest heartache.

The best teachers concerning this point are those who have made the worst mistakes – mistakes that cost them the gravest heartache. David, as a result, might be the best teacher on the subject.

Second Samuel chapter twelve references the aftermath of David's biggest blunder. Nathan, the prophet of God, has already pointed his bony finger at David and said, "Thou art the man." Remember the story? Read what happens afterwards.

God strikes the health of Bathsheba's infant. We find David fasting, praying, and begging God to change His mind and to heal David's dying child.

David knows very well that his sin has brought this upon a little innocent baby. David knew that he should have gone to war when all the kings went forth to battle.

I guarantee you that if David could have changed one day in his life, he would go back to that day. He would go to the day that he gave the order to his armies to march from the comfort of his home – not from on his horse or from in his chariot. He would change it all.

I guarantee you that if David could have changed one day, it would have been that same night when he went up to his roof and could not sleep. He was restless. I believe the devil was probably stirring him, luring him out on the rooftop. If David could change what resulted, he would. If he could just change one day...

If you could just change one day, does a day come to mind?

You made a horrible decision, and you knew better. That one decision has snowballed into a life of heartache. You have had to go through the school of life the hard way because of that one decision and what resulted.

May I give you some encouragement? Who you *were* back then does not have to be who you *are* today. Greater is He that is in me than He that is in the world.8 We can thank God for His grace and mercy. He has given us an unlimited amount of second chances. He does not remember our sins anymore.

There are some things that we have *absolutely no control over*. Circumstances rear their ugly head sometimes because of past sin and sometimes not from sin at all. So, of the things we do have control over, let us choose to do right. Of the things we can choose, let us choose Christ.

My wife has been driving me all around town. As my personal chauffer, she calls herself "The Green Sedan." I cannot drive anywhere by myself. I text her, and she comes. If I ask her, "Can you take me over here?" and she says no, there is not much I can do about it! As I have mentioned before, my wife and I have grown closer through all of this. We spend a lot of time together. She helps me with getting out of bed and driving across town. The point is that the situation is out of my control.

Some trials we go through require determination on our part to make it without knowing for sure what the lesson is. We find ourselves asking God, "Lord, if You would only tell me what I am supposed to be learning here, and I will be good." What if God never shows me why I am going through what I am going through? What if I never get the proper use of my right

---

8 See I John 4:4

leg back and I never find out why I went through it all? What if I forever have this burning pain inside of it? Am I going to quit next month because I think God is not faithful? I sincerely hope not.

It could be that we *never* know the reason for the lesson here on earth. It could be that when I breathe my last breath here and I take my first breath up there, that my Saviour might tell me the answer. As I am looking square into the eyes of my Saviour, His answer might be, "I just wanted to see if you would make it. I wanted to see if you could stand in front of a bunch of people every week and tell them they have to make it, too. If that is the case, then I want to make sure I pass the test.

I have determined that I am not going to shake my fist at God. I am not going to threaten Him by saying, "All right, Lord, teach me what this lesson is all about or I'm going to quit!" Though we cannot change the circumstance, though we cannot control the circumstance, though we may not enjoy the circumstance, we can accept it.

God has a plan, and He has gotten me this far. I am 35 years old at the time of this writing, and I am still alive and kicking. I am making it. Maybe I can go for another 35 years.

Are your prayers filled with question marks? Have you found yourself in a quitting place because of sin or not because of any sin at all? Are you fine with

God not giving you an answer this side of glory? If your situation is outside of your control, are you comfortable with it being in God's control?

FINISHING OUR COURSE

A S WE CONCLUDE this section, I leave you again with my life's verse, Acts 20:24: "But none of these things move me, neither count I my life dear unto myself, so that I might finish my course..."

I certainly want to finish right. How about you? It is going to take some determination, is it not?

If we ever get to the point of thinking about quitting on Christ, may we purpose in our hearts to make it through that quitting place. May we be surrendered enough so that we can learn what the Lord is trying to teach us. Let us go into every day with the prayer, "Lord, whatever You want to teach me today, I want to learn it."

I may not be happy with my pain. I might not enjoy the pain. You might not enjoy your pain. Nevertheless, because of Christ, we still have reason to smile. We still have reason to finish. We still have reason to learn what we can.

PART V

LOVING JESUS

"Beloved, let us love one another: for love is of God; and every one that loveth is born of God, and knoweth God."
—*I JOHN 4:7*

THE INTRODUCTION TO OUR CONCLUSION

OUR FINAL LESSON TOGETHER is the most decisive one. Without this last ingredient, there can be no endurance during the quitting place. You and I will fail without it. We have studied where we need to be *looking*, to whom we need to be *listening*, what we need to be *letting go*, and what we need to be *learning*. Our fifth and final thought, though, makes all the difference.

One thing I notice is that all of us go through quitting places at different times and at different intervals. We will *all* go through these quitting places many times over in our life and for different reasons.

Employees want to quit their jobs from time to time. Most of the time, a person quits in the *heat of the moment*, with an *irrational mindset*, and in a *hasty manner*. An employee will walk out on his job on

Tuesday because he finally was fed up. Then on Wednesday, the employee reflects and *regrets*.

I have met men and women who have quit on their marriages. A month goes by after they have given up and they wake up wondering, "What in the world have I done?"

There will be times when you want to quit being a parent. To the expecting mothers, there are probably times where you want to quit carrying your child (for a little while anyway).

I have observed children who have run away from homes. They quit when times got tough. All of a sudden, after they are done with their pity party and done with being angry at mom and dad, they ask themselves, "What in the world did I just do?" Some of you readers have been there. You know exactly what I am talking about.

We are privileged here at Calvary Baptist Church to have a Reformers Unanimous program. God has used us to help many of the addicted. Sometimes, a person who has been clean for three, four, five, and even ten years falls off the wagon. Something bad happens, and they find themselves doing what has taken them ten years to work toward not doing. They did not make it through the quitting place. When they come to themselves, they feel ashamed – like the prodigal son in the hog pen when "he came to himself."

These situations remind us of Nebuchadnezzar, whom we studied in the past section of this book. He came to himself. Reasoning returned. He wished he had done what he knew to be right.

Again, the quitting places come to us *all*. For a variety of reasons. In a variety of ways. Quitting places are inevitable.

The quitting places come in a pastor's life, and the quitting places come in the people's lives. The quitting places are going to come in a nation's life – whether it is our nation of America or a country in Africa. You can try to run from it, but wherever you end up running to, there will be a quitting place there, too.

The purpose of saying that is not to scare you, to make you paranoid, or to make you a pessimist. It is to admonish you that wherever you are when a quitting place comes, to *plant yourself.* Apply godly principles (some of which are found in this book), and do not run.

Half the time, the reason we quit is because we feel like we were not treated fairly. Every reader of this book will say at some point in life, "This isn't fair."

There are circumstances in life that truly *are not* fair. You worked hard and you lost your job anyway. That really is not fair. "It is not fair I have to grow up in a separated home," a teenager or child says. That really is not fair. "I am serving God and I am doing everything God wants me to do, and I still feel like nothing is going right. It's just not fair," you find yourself saying. As long as you cling to the "That's not fair" attitude, all of life is going to be pretty disappointing. At some point, we *must* learn to make it through the quitting place. There must come a time when we pray a submitted prayer to God, "Lord, if this is what you want, then I am in it for the long haul."

Someone once said that when life gives you lemons, make lemonade. It is what you do with what comes your way that matters.

Without deciding to make it through, no matter what, life spirals out of control. You find yourself going to work with the "Woe is me" mentality – displaying what Christianity is "really" about to an unsaved workplace. You find yourself receiving counsel from your coworkers that do not even know Christ. You start taking their marriage counsel over your pastor's marriage counsel. "Well, you know, there's more fish in the pond if you are not happy with your mate," they say. Hold on a second. You might be married for years and have two children. Why would you go looking for a fish in another pond? There will be a quitting place once you have netted the fish from the other pond as well! While the grass might be greener on the other side of the fence, you still have to mow that grass, too!

Stick it out. Make it through. Now is not the time to quit.

But how? *That* is the reason you are reading this book, is it not?

To be very straightforward with you, there might not be a step 1, 2, 3 solution for your situation. There is, however, something that you *must have* in order to make it through your quitting place. The remaining pages of this book are dedicated to this very thing. If you and I are going to make it through our quitting place, we are going to have to make sure that we are *loving Jesus*.

THE DEFINITION OF GOD

NEVER STOP loving Jesus. He never stops loving us. The most bountiful text on the love of God in the Bible might very well be First John chapter four. In it, we find what God's love really is and why God's love is so important during our quitting place. Take the time to read the following verses as we jump into this important subject.

I John 4:7 Beloved, let us love one another: for love is of God; and every one that loveth is born of God, and knoweth God.

[8] He that loveth not knoweth not God; for God is love.

[9] In this was manifested the love of God toward us, because that God sent his only begotten Son into the world, that we might live through him.

[10] Herein is love, not that we loved God, but that he loved us, and sent his Son to be the propitiation for our sins.

[11] Beloved, if God so loved us, we ought also to love one another.

[12] No man hath seen God at any time. If we love one another, God dwelleth in us, and his love is perfected in us.

[13] Hereby know we that we dwell in him, and he in us, because he hath given us of his Spirit.

[14] And we have seen and do testify that the Father sent the Son to be the Saviour of the world.

[15] Whosoever shall confess that Jesus is the Son of God, God dwelleth in him, and he in God.

[16] And we have known and believed the love that God hath to us. God is love; and he that dwelleth in love dwelleth in God, and God in him.

[17] Herein is our love made perfect, that we may have boldness in the day of judgment: because as he is, so are we in this world.

[18] There is no fear in love; but perfect love casteth out fear: because fear hath torment. He that feareth is not made perfect in love.

[19] We love him, because he first loved us.

[20] If a man say, I love God, and hateth his brother, he is a liar: for he that loveth not his brother whom he hath seen, how can he love God whom he hath not seen?

[21] And this commandment have we from him, That he who loveth God love his brother also.

God is love. I have preached for years that the definition of love is God, and the definition of God is love. You will hear people say, "I don't understand love." God's response to man in First John is that you will never fully understand love until you first put your faith and trust in the Son of God.

You can never fully understand what love is until love is made manifest by the way of the Spirit of God in your life.[9] Only then can God become real to you. Only then is God more than merely a word taken in vain. He becomes more than a lifeless idol on a shelf – that is not the kind of God we have available to us.

The God I have loves me, even when I am not lovable. He promised to never leave me nor forsake me. That is a wonderful promise. It is also a wonderful challenge to us. Why? People hurt us all the time, do

---

they not? God is careful not to write us off, and we should be careful not to write others off also.

It took the prodigal son a while to come to himself. We are not sure exactly how long, but it took him a while. It took Nebuchadnezzar seven years, roaming as the beast in the field...but then the Lord restored his kingdom. It took David some time before he went to God and said, "Restore to me the joy of thy salvation."[10] Throughout all of these situations and our situations, too, God never stops working and He never stops loving us!

God loves us even when He has to take us through difficult times. He acts as our heavenly parent, showing love in a way parents must show love. There will be times (or there are times right now) that you feel that God does not love you or that He has forgotten all about you. Just hold on for a little while longer. Time will prove His love for you.

---

[10] See Psalm 51:12

IF YOU LOVE ME...

MOSES CAME SO CLOSE to the Promised Land. It seems like he came too close not to have made it in. No, the Promised Land does not represent Heaven, lest we get the idea through the children of Israel's example that we can eventually work our way into Heaven. The Promised Land represents the victorious Christian life that we can experience. The Promised Land is what lies on the other side of the quitting place – victory and victorious living. That is what I want. What about you?

Even in the Promised Land, there are battles. Praise the Lord, there will be no more battles in Heaven! However, while I am here on Earth, I can decide what side of Jordan I live on – in the wilderness or in the Promised Land.

Moses caught a glimpse of the Promised Land – the land of victory. He did not get to cross over, though. If we are not careful ourselves, we can come so close, and miss victory by an inch.

God brought Moses to the top of a mount to show him everything Moses could have had – all the blessings he would never enjoy. Why the defeat? Why would there be no victory after that whole journey?

There was a time when God looked at Moses and basically said, "I want you to take your staff and smite the rock." Moses did, and the water gushed forth. Then there came a time when the people were murmuring. God told Moses to speak to the rock this time instead of smiting it. Moses was so fed up with the murmuring of the children of Israel that he took his staff and hit the rock twice. He disobeyed in a moment of anger.

Because of his action, God told Moses that he would not be allowed into the Promised Land. Moses said his goodbyes to his family, and then made his way up to a mountain, never to return. I wonder how Moses felt when he saw how close he was – when he knew he had let God down.

So, what caused Moses to not have victory? He disobeyed. So, what could Moses have done differently? John 14:15 gives us the answer, "If ye love me, keep my commandments." We demonstrate our love to God by keeping His commandments. Disobeying God demonstrates to Him that we do not love Him. Therefore, if we love God, we will make it a priority to keep His commandments. Moses would have experienced victory had he obeyed. The same is true for our obedience to God. *Loving God* is the key to keeping His will. Disobedience takes away our victory.

According to the world, you may have every reason and every right to quit in your quitting place. You may think you have every reason to throw in the towel and say, "You know what? I am *done!*"

Would it not be sad if you quit the night before the Lord comes back? If His second coming is as imminent as we preach and believe, why in the world would we consider quitting a night before possibly being called into glory?

We need to remind ourselves in the moment we are tempted to disobey (proving our lack of love for Christ) to resist the devil. We are *promised* that if we resist, he *will* flee.[11] Maybe we ought to try it sometime. Put your fist up to the devil and say, "You know what? I am not coming to you with my own strength. I am coming to you in the power of the Lord." Prove your love to God by not hastily indulging in disobedience in the heat of the moment. Your Promised Land of victory is worth it.

---

[11] See James 4:7

WORDS VS. ACTIONS

J ESUS HAS NEVER STOPPED loving you. Whether a person has been out of church for five years – whether he is still in the hog pen or coming back from the hog pen – Jesus will not stop loving him. We, on the other hand, have a tendency to stop showing our love toward Christ.

I have often heard people who are no longer serving the Lord say, "I never stopped loving Jesus." I would like to reply to this person who tells me this, while they are holding a Budweiser in one hand and a cigarette in the other, "How is your life telling Jesus that you love Him? How do your actions say I love you when you are not in His house, in His Word, or doing His will?"

It is like a husband who one day decides he wants to leave his family. Without any notice, he abandons his wife and children. He does not show up for two years. He does not write home. He does not call to tell his wife happy anniversary or to tell his kids happy birthday. No phone call, no text message, no email, no Facebook, no Twitter, no carrier pigeon. Then, he shows up after two years have gone by and says, "Hey Honey, I am here. I love you." He walks into the house as though he was never gone. I think that wife is probably going to say, "Whoa! whoa! Get out. Who are you?"

"Well, I am your husband," he responds.

"No. No. I know who you are. But who *are* you? The husband that I used to know wouldn't have left me for two years without so much as a word. I mean, I didn't know where you went. I didn't know if you were with someone else," she replies.

As bizarre as this imaginary story is, we act like we could do that to God and everything will be all right. It is true that God will forgive at a moment's notice if all we do is ask for forgiveness. I am in no way arguing that. I am concentrating more on the aspect of showing God we love Him. Abandoning our relationship with God does not show Him love.

"Even though I quit, I never stopped loving him." Really?

Let me tell you what brings a man home every night: love. Let me tell you what compels me to pray with my children every night: love. Let me tell you what compels me to discipline my children when they do wrong: love. Let me tell you what makes me want to hug my wife, kiss her, and say I love you: love. We demonstrate our love through action, not through empty wordplay.

If we are not careful, we treat God with about as much disrespect as many people treat their next-door neighbors – never greeting them because you are too busy. But, when you need to borrow something from them or when you need a favor, you knock on their door. Try that speech on them: "I know I have always been too busy to talk to you, but I want to let you know that I have never stopped loving you."

Let us not treat God that way. He does not treat us that way. He longs for a personal relationship. The Holy Spirit woos us. Christ has demonstrated His love toward us. He continues to show His love toward us. Is it too much of Him to ask for demonstrations of love from you?

I Never Moved

H E HAD BEEN REFURBISHING the old car for some time. The old bench-style seats had been faded and torn with age, but the elderly husband now had the car looking like new. Finally, it was ready to take his wife for a ride.

The couple had spent many, many hours riding in that old car. As they were riding down the road in it, the wife started getting a bit nostalgic. They had been married for years. All the kids were now reared and now had families of their own. Driving in that old car brought back so many memories.

The lady looked over at her husband across the bench seat and said, "Do you remember all the memories we had riding in this car? I would sit there right next to you, hip-to-hip. You would put your arm around me and we would have long, romantic drives."

"Yes, I remember," he said.

something. When I asked him how he was doing, he said, "Well, I am down here under the bus right now, so I only have a minute."

I am grateful for that. He had every reason in the world to quit. He went through about a year and a half where he could not even drive a car. He cannot drive a bus, but he works on them anyway.

There have been times when the elevator at the church has been broken. There he is at the church with his tools, helping to fix it. Why? For one, he has to be able to get upstairs somehow. But really, he wants to be a blessing, and this is a way that he can serve.

The reason I do not want to quit is not because I am such a strong guy. I have a father who is a great example to me.

I also have a Father who is an example to me. We all do.

There will come a time when we tell our children the stories of all the tough times. For now, let us let them *see* us make it. Let us not just talk about it.

Growing up, I watched my mom and dad not quit. My mom and dad never burdened us down by explaining all of the issues that were going on. As a kid, though, I could sense it when times were tough. I observed them as they kept on going.

Now it means so much when I can reflect on those times with my parents. They will begin to talk about some of the heartaches they went through and how they made it. I am so grateful that they made it when they could have quit. It means more to me at 35 than it ever did at fifteen.

Seeing an example helps us. To know what Jesus did for me, to know that He did not quit, to know how deeply He loved me, gives me an example. It gives me hope that I can make it, too.

YOKED UP

J ESUS SHOWS ME His love in so many ways. One specific way He shows me His love is in Matthew Chapter eleven.

It is a lovely thought to think that Christ carries me through the difficult times. I think of that beautiful poem, "Footprints in the Sand," and I know many have read its lines about Jesus walking with us on the shores of time. The poem goes on to say that the reason there was only one set of footprints in the sand during the difficult times is that, during those times, Jesus was carrying us.

Though I love the poem, I do not know if it is correct when compared to what Jesus taught. I find that Jesus describes the situation a little differently. Let us read:

Matthew 11:28: Come unto me, all ye that labour and are heavy laden, and I will give you rest.

[29] Take my yoke upon you, and learn of me; for I am meek and lowly in heart: and ye shall find rest unto your souls.

[30] For my yoke is easy, and my burden is light.

If the Footprints poem is right, that would mean that there comes a time in my life where the Lord takes my head out of the yoke, throws me up on His back, and He keeps plowing by Himself. I do not think that is true. The reason is that He says, "For my yoke is easy, and my burden is light." (Matthew 11:30) No, the burden (yoke) does not go away. However, Jesus offers the tired plowman the chance to yoke up with Him. Working alongside of Jesus and allowing him to shoulder our burden with us makes it easy and light.

If life is so unbearable, maybe you have your head in the wrong yoke. He promised to never leave me or forsake me. I cannot find where He promised that He would carry me, though.

The day is coming when He is going to give me a horse to carry me. I will be in Heaven at that time – getting to ride with Jesus. That is going to be a great day. Until then, Jesus requests that I work alongside of Him.

When Elijah found Elisha, there Elisha was, plowing as if he was one of the cattle with his head in the yoke. I do not know where that other ox was that day; but for whatever reason, the ox could not plow. I picture Elisha as this big hulk of a man with the attitude, "Nothing is going to keep me from plowing this field, not even if I have to plow it myself as one of the animals." So he put his head in that twelfth yoke. Elisha knew the job needed to be done. It was his burden to bear.

I ask you, reader, "Is your head in the right yoke?" There are going to be burdens. That is certain. If you have had a life of ease up until now, then you are not living the same Christian life that I am living.

When the burdens come your way, you do not make it because you are Superman. I am certainly not going to make it because I am Superman. I am not making it because I am a better Christian than anybody else. I am not. I am wrapped in the same flesh that everyone else is. I go through ups and downs, and sometimes there are far more downs than I want there to be. The only reason that I have made it thus far is that Jesus has been with me all the way – shouldering the load that I cannot bear alone.

It is harder to plow a field when it is you doing the work. Are you trying to do it all by yourself? I bet it would be easier on you if you took on Jesus' yoke.

One thing that I have noticed about oxen is that they are always looking down when they plow. They are not looking far off into the distance or looking around them at the other oxen.

Our problem, sometimes, is that we try bearing our burden and plowing the field while looking around at everyone else. If I am gawking at how everyone else is doing his work, that is going to mess up my work. I think that the Lord sometimes slaps our heads back down and says, "I don't want you to see how Brother so and so is doing. Pay attention to what you have to do." Why? Because if you are looking around, your nice straight lines are going to start to become crooked. Before you know it, you are going to run into some fences. You are going to do more damage than you are good. God wants us to focus on our own task at hand instead of comparing ourselves with how others are doing.

Just stay steady. Stop looking at everybody else's field. If you are yoked up with Christ and they are yoked up with Christ, you both will be able to make it through the quitting place.

Keep plowing your field, but make sure your head is in the right yoke.

LOVE BY LISTENING

I WILL NEVER FORGET my times of playing baseball as a teenager. We were going into pre-college ball, and our coaches were doing everything they could to make us better. I found that *when I listened to my coaches*, I improved. They cared about making me better than I was.

They started to teach us how to stand in the batter's box. They showed us that when we opened up our stance we could see the hand of the pitcher as he delivered the ball. As the pitcher turned his body a little bit, you could learn to watch that ball to discern what kind of pitch was heading your way. We learned to watch the spin on the ball. You could tell if the pitch was going to be a sinker, or a curve ball, or a slider. You could tell if the ball might hit you or not.

I remember after all those lessons, many of our batting averages improved. When we started listening to someone who knew better, we started performing better. We wanted to listen. We did not want to strike out.

They taught us how to properly steal a base. Though I cannot steal a base anymore because of my leg problem, I still retain what those coaches taught me. They taught me that when you are stealing a base, always keep your body mass in the center. We were to be on the balls of our feet so that we could rock forward a little bit, but not too much as to lose balance. They taught us to keep our eyes on the pitcher's feet. As long as we were watching the pitcher's feet, while our peripheral vision could see the whole pitcher, we could tell if he was going to try to throw us out or not. If the pitcher was right handed, his back foot would start to step off, and he would have to spin around fast. Now, if he is going to throw you out over at third base, he cannot telegraph any movement toward home plate. He has to throw straight toward that third base. My coaches knew what they were talking about. By listening and incorporating what they taught, I became a better player.

I will never forget when I was taking kickboxing. I would be in the ring getting nailed all the time – getting knocked around and knocked out. Finally, the coach came over to me and said, "It has been three weeks of you trying to do your own thing in the ring.

Are you ready to listen?" I was tired of getting hurt. I said, "Yes sir."

So, he started teaching, and I started listening. "Keep your eye on their chest. Watch their chest when you are in the ring," he said. Up until that point, I had been watching my opponent's eyes. It is difficult to tell when a person is going to throw his first punch if you are looking at his eyes.

My coach taught me how to get my arm up to block. He taught me how to throw a jab. He showed me how some right-handed boxers could switch to be left-handed boxers and that the left hand could be just as powerful as the right hand.

I learned that my teacher was right. He knew what he was talking about. Whenever the opponent was getting ready to punch, his chest muscles would tense up, telling me to get ready.

I learned quickly that you do not hold your elbow out when you are boxing. Your hands should be right in front...unless you want to end up on your back in a matter of two seconds.

When I was tired of being hurt, I had no problem listening.

If we would listen to the God of the Book, we would perform better. I am tired of getting to the end of a boxing match with the devil, and I am the one that lost.

The Lord, the One Who beat the devil, is trying to tell me, "Resist. That is his weakness. *I know*."

The best way to show people how to do something is not doing it for them. It is doing it *with* them. The coach cannot play for the player, but he can teach the player. It is our job to listen. Those who love, listen. Those who do not love, do not.

THE APPROVAL PROCESS

T HERE ARE MANY SITUATIONS that I find myself in that I do not love. However, since I know that every situation I face passes through the approval process of the Lord, then He must know that I can handle the situation I am facing. I might not love the situation, *but I do love the Lord.*

I can only do my part. When I do my part, God promises that He will do His. If I am 1) Trusting in the Lord with all my heart, 2) Leaning not on my own understanding, and 3) In all my ways acknowledging Him, He *will* direct my path.[12]

If I love him, I believe through faith that everything He allows to come my way is approved by Him. He must know that I can handle the situations that I am facing. If I believe He approved it, I am going to trust Him enough to see me through it.

---

[12] See Proverbs 3:5

By the way, God knows your situation, too. He approved it. Trust Him. He will see your through it.

First Corinthians 10:13 gives a wonderful promise to us. The verse says, "There hath no temptation taken you but such as is common to man: but God is faithful, who will not suffer you to be tempted above that ye are able; *but will with the temptation also make a way to escape, that ye may be able to bear it.*" (Emphases added)

If you will allow me to paraphrase that verse: God will never give you more than you can handle.

You might be saying, "I can't take anymore." Somewhere along the line, you missed the way to escape. God provided it. If you are in a quitting place right now and you feel like you cannot go any further, it might be because you have not been walking with Him.

He said that He will never give you more than you can bear. He will never give me more. He will never give any of us more than we can handle.

Loving Jesus is displayed by respecting His approval process. If He has entrusted me with the problem that I find myself in, then I am going to trust Him enough to get me through it. How about you?

CONCLUSION

I HAD THE PRIVILEGE of being reared in a Christian home. I watched my parent's lives inside and outside of the home, and I found their Christian lives to be genuine. I say that to say this – I have had many great examples in my life that have showed that with Christ all things are possible.

As I said earlier in this book, I remember when Dr. Larry Brown made the statement, "We have to learn to make it through the quitting places." It was at a Pastor's and Workers Conference in Santa Clara, California. I was a college student at the time, and that statement stuck in my heart.

My prayer and desire is that people do not ever look at me and think, "What a strong man of God he is!" I am absolutely nothing without the Lord. Throughout my life I have been amazed at how true, genuine strength comes from the Lord over and over again. He is always faithful, and His words do not return void. I pray that this book encourages people to keep looking unto Jesus (Psalm 121), and that together we will continue to press toward the mark!

I have never loved Jesus more than I do right now. I pray that my love for Him will continue to grow and deepen until I reach the splendors of Heaven. His strength is made perfect in our weakness! I never truly understood that statement until my cancer. Oh, I would have told you before that I understood what it meant. However, it took God bringing me to a place where all I could do was turn toward Him for strength; that helped me to understand a little bit better what the Apostle Paul was saying. I have not "arrived," but I can tell you this, "I am enjoying the journey a whole lot better since cancer than I ever thought possible."

As I close, may I encourage you to just keep on keeping on for the cause of Christ. When you are emotionally low, when you are discouraged, when the bad news keeps rolling in, and when it seems like it cannot get any worse – remember that God has promised to never leave us nor forsake us. He is that Friend that sticks closer than a brother! His ways are perfect! I am saved and on my way to Heaven – *forever*! Through Bible reading and prayer I can discover again and again how I can make it through the quitting places in life!